"Lamia and Krieger have hit the nail on the head by identifying a major problem in contemporary relationships—the compulsive need to rescue. Their book, *The White Knight Syndrome*, clearly articulates the dynamics of this all-too-common pattern. This book is an outstanding resource and a must-read for every compulsive rescuer, as well as for mental health students and professionals."

> —Ronald F. Levant, Ed.D., past president of the American Psychological Association and professor of psychology at Buchtel College of Arts and Sciences at the University of Akron in Akron, OH

"This book is aimed at anyone who recognizes that the white knight syndrome may explain feelings of betrayal, anger, or guilt. Because the book does such a good job with explaining the complex emotional lives of rescuers, it can be a great resource for therapists as well as clients."

> —Michael J. Garanzini, S.J., Ph.D., president of Loyola University in Chicago, IL, and author of *Child-Centered Schools* and *The Attachment Cycle*

"The authors of *The White Knight Syndrome* are experienced and insightful clinicians. Building on their extensive professional work as psychotherapists, they have delivered a compelling, concise, and highly useful delineation of a repetitive but maladaptive pattern of needing to compulsively rescue others. Moreover, they show how to move forward in life to an adaptive pattern they call a balanced rescuer: a person who cares, preserves intimacy, and also develops even more self-esteem. I enthusiastically recommend this outstanding book."

> —Mardi Horowitz, MD, president of the San Francisco Center for Psychoanalysis, professor of psychiatry at the University of California, San Francisco, and author of *A Course in Happiness*

"*The White Knight Syndrome* is unique among psychology books because it is so well-written. The case descriptions are engaging, and the 'Thinking About It' sections brilliantly incorporate the reader's experience into the dialogue so that the material presented becomes personally relevant. *The White Knight Syndrome* is a great piece of work."

—Sylvia Boorstein, Ph.D., psychotherapist and founding teacher and Spirit Rock Meditation Center in Woodacre, CA, author of *It's Easier Than You Think and Happiness Is an Inside Job*

The
White
Knight
Syndrome

Rescuing Yourself from Your Need to Rescue Others

MARY C. LAMIA, PH.D.
MARILYN J. KRIEGER, PH.D.

New Harbinger Publications, Inc.

Publisher's Note

This publication is designed to provide accurate and authoritative information in regard to the subject matter covered. It is sold with the understanding that the publisher is not engaged in rendering psychological, financial, legal, or other professional services. If expert assistance or counseling is needed, the services of a competent professional should be sought.

Distributed in Canada by Raincoast Books

Cover design by Amy Shoup; Text design by Michele Waters-Kermes; Acquired by Melissa Kirk; Edited by Kayla Sussell

Library of Congress Cataloging in Publication Data on file

Printed in the United States of America

Library of Congress Cataloging-in-Publication Data

Lamia, Mary C.
  The white knight syndrome : rescuing yourself from your need to rescue others / Mary C. Lamia and Marilyn J. Krieger.
    p. cm.
  Includes bibliographical references.
  ISBN-13: 978-1-57224-624-9 (pbk. : alk. paper)
  ISBN-10: 1-57224-624-3 (pbk. : alk. paper)
  1. Couples--Psychology. 2. Need (Psychology) 3. Helping behavior. 4. Man-woman relationships. 5. Interpersonal relations. I. Krieger, Marilyn J. II. Title.
HQ801.L276 2009
177'.7--dc22
                          2009007132

FSC

Mixed Sources

Product group from well-managed forests and other controlled sources

Cert no. SW-COC-002283
www.fsc.org
© 1996 Forest Stewardship Council

11   10   09

10   9   8   7   6   5   4   3   2   1   First printing

To our husbands, of course

Contents

Acknowledgments

We are indebted to Matthew McKay for the opportunity to have our book be a part of the New Harbinger collection. Gratitude is owed to Kayla Sussell, Melissa Kirk, and Jess Beebe for their suggestions and overall support. We want to thank our students and colleagues who over the years have shared their cases with us. We will express individual and personal recognition to several of them whose names are withheld in the interest of confidentiality. Appreciation is lovingly due our husbands, our children and their partners, and our friends for their input, enthusiasm, and understanding as we immersed ourselves in this process. And we certainly want to acknowledge the individuals and couples who have trusted us with their stories and lives. Finally, we are overwhelmingly grateful for our friendship of many years and delighted to be on these pages together.

Introduction

Sir Lancelot, Wonder Woman, and Superman are examples of the classic white knight: the selfless, strong, resourceful man or woman who arrives at the last moment to save the innocent and helpless from dragons, crime, or evildoers. The term *white knight* as the name for rescuers has been in use since medieval times. An archetype in legends and folklore, the white knight is an attractive, romantic, and powerful figure. In literature, plays, movies, and songs we find many who wish to be a white knight or those who say they need one.

The Contemporary White Knight

A white knight can be a woman or man of any age, race, sexual orientation, culture, or socioeconomic status. The contemporary real-life white knight may appear to be a gem of a partner but is actually a tragic hero. White knights demonstrate not only a willingness but also a need to rescue. In fact, often without self-awareness, white knights seek out as partners those who are especially needy or vulnerable. Thus, in our conceptualization of the white knight syndrome, the inclination and the need to rescue are the fundamental requirements for white knighthood.

Take a few moments to consider the various relationships you know about or those in which you've been involved. It's likely you know of relationships that include people who have found partners in need of rescuing—the rescue could have been from anything—unhappiness, financial chaos, substance abuse, depression, an abusive relationship, medical issues, or a past that left them wounded. Perhaps the rescuers you know intuitively recognized their partners' core neediness or vulnerability, regardless of how well disguised that person's weakness was at the beginning of their relationship.

You will discover that many rescuers often go from one person in need of rescue to another, riding into each new partner's life on a white horse to save the day. In the initial stages of the relationship, the rescuer seems gracious and happily altruistic, but as time goes by, he feels increasingly unhappy, disappointed, critical, and powerless. These are our white knights. Although a white knight can exist in a wide range of relationships, such as in a business or a friendship, for the purposes of our book we will focus on the white knight in intimate relationships.

Behind the Motivation to Rescue

What motivates the white knight to rescue her partner? The answer lies in understanding her goals for being in the relationship in the first place, goals that may be beyond her awareness. Although the white knight's heroic actions may take the form of slaying her partner's metaphorical dragons, her real goal involves slaying the dragons from her own past. The white knight hopes to receive admiration, validation, or love from her partner. Yet at a deeper level the compulsive rescuer is trying to repair the negative or damaged sense of herself that developed in childhood.

Unfortunately, the white knight's choice of a partner, and how that partner is eventually treated, often repeats symbolically the very same kind of distress that the white knight himself experienced in childhood. Rather than repairing his sense of self, this repetition leaves the white knight feeling defeated. Until the white knight truly understands his motives, his quest for self-healing through perpetual rescuing is destined to result in unhappiness and failure.

Who This Book Is For

An understanding of the white knight syndrome will help you achieve a greater understanding of your own compulsive rescuing or the rescuing behavior of another person. By offering general discussions and case examples, we will provide you with a model you can use to assess any unhealthy tendencies you may have to rescue other people. We'll explore the dynamics that give rise to the white knight syndrome and the relationships that typically evolve. This new understanding will help you to move beyond the choices and repetitive patterns that prevent you from forming healthy relationships and keep you unfulfilled.

The insights we provide can serve as the first step toward healing yourself and help you create relationships with true emotional depth and warmth. When you can give up knighthood and become a balanced rescuer, you will be free to find a true and worthy partner.

Why We Wrote This Book

As psychologists, each with more than thirty years' experience, we found that we had worked with many men and women upon whom we've now bestowed the title of white knight. Typically, these people repeatedly found partners who needed rescuing from some life difficulty. When we described the concept of the white knight syndrome to those who fit the typical pattern, they identified with the prototype and adopted the term to describe themselves or the behavior of others.

Although recognizing a problem is the first step in solving it, these self-identified white knights also needed to understand the origins of their actions, disengage from their old patterns, and develop new ways of thinking about their relationships and partners. If you are a white knight, we hope the material in this book will help you to better understand your own relationship dynamics and lead you to make better choices in your intimate relationships.

What This Book Covers

The first chapter explores in greater detail our definition of the white knight syndrome, provides an overview of the different subtypes of white knights, and introduces the concept of the balanced rescuer. In chapter 2, we review the early life experiences and psychological mechanisms that give rise to the white knight syndrome. Chapter 3 discusses basic theories of altruism and empathy, and clarifies the differences and similarities between the wish to help and the white knight syndrome. Chapter 4 explores why and how the white knight protects herself or himself. Chapters 5 through 7 present detailed cases and analyses for each of the white knight subtypes that are introduced in chapter 1: the overly empathic white knight, the tarnished white knight, and the terrorizing/terrified white knight. Chapter 8 provides ways to think about and understand the partners whom white knights typically choose. Chapter 9 describes two cases that demonstrate healthy rescuing in a well-functioning relationship. Chapter 10 offers guidelines for self-reflection to help you begin rescuing yourself from your need to rescue others. Each chapter ends with a set of questions designed to aid you in thinking more deeply about the ideas presented in that chapter.

Throughout the book we provide case examples from our clinical practice and those of our colleagues, as well as interviews with ordinary people who have experienced a "rescuing" relationship. All identifying information about these white knights, balanced rescuers, and their partners has been changed. Note that all of the cases presented in this book are composites. That is, when several people had similar situations and dynamics, we combined their stories into one case to further disguise their identities. We alternate between using male and female examples throughout the book.

Let's Begin

You now have a general understanding of the *white knight syndrome:* a compulsive need to be the rescuer in an intimate relationship originating from early life experiences that left the white knight feeling damaged, shamed, or afraid. Take a look at the following questionnaire and see what resonates with you. Note your answers so that you can refer back to them when they are reviewed at the end of chapter 1.

Questionnaire: Are You a White Knight?

Decide whether the following statements are mostly true or false for you.

	True	False
1. My partner made me feel idolized in the beginning of our relationship.	____	____
2. I have to be extremely watchful of what I say or do, lest I upset or anger my partner.	____	____
3. I feel that the responsibility of managing my life, together with my partner's, all rests on me.	____	____
4. I have stayed in relationships out of a sense of guilt or worry about my partner.	____	____
5. At the start of the relationship, I saw my partner as dangerously exciting or exotic.	____	____
6. Often, I know better than my partner what is best for him or her.	____	____
7. People don't realize that I am extremely self-critical.	____	____
8. I often disregard my own needs to focus on just my partner's needs.	____	____
9. I often feel that my partner doesn't appreciate all that I do for him or her.	____	____
10. I look back on many of my relationships and realize I have been rescuing my partners.	____	____

1

White Knight Basics

White knights have a compulsive need to rescue, but how and why they rescue can be quite varied. This chapter will give you an overview of the basic characteristics common to all white knights and the variance among them. Four subtypes of rescuers will be introduced: the overly empathic white knight, the tarnished white knight, the terrorizing/terrified white knight, and the balanced rescuer. You will learn a great deal more about these four subtypes in later chapters. We end this chapter with a summary of the white knight syndrome and a discussion of answers to the questionnaire that appeared in the introduction.

White Knight Commonalities

White knights treat their partners altruistically, but their altruistic endeavors often represent a struggle with their own internal conflicts, as well as a way of staying close to their partners. Does this mean that the white knight's rescuing behavior is not truly altruistic? This complex question will be addressed later in the book. For now, we will focus on the white knight's conscious helping behavior and consider it as altruistic.

White knights often have a history of loss, abandonment, trauma, or unrequited love. Many of them were deeply affected by the emotional or physical suffering of a caregiver. In our work with white knights we've found them to be emotionally sensitive and vulnerable, traits that cause them to be hurt easily by others.

Empathy, the ability to understand and identify with the feelings of another, is a highly developed character trait of all white knights. The white knight's ability to put herself into another person's shoes can be used either to help or, unfortunately, to control or hurt her partner. We discuss empathy in more detail in later chapters.

After carefully reviewing the cases that met our definition of a white knight, we created a list of traits and behaviors that characterize the white knight. Typically, white knights have a history that includes many of the following:

- Self-defeating behavior that may involve substance abuse

- Heightened awareness in childhood of a parent's hardships

- Childhood neglect

- Childhood emotional, physical, or sexual abuse

- Loss or threat of loss of a significant caregiver in childhood

- Repeatedly finding partners who need rescuing

A white knight typically has many of the following character traits:

- Fears emotional distance

- Is very emotionally vulnerable and sensitive

- Has a tendency to idealize the partner

- Has an extreme need to be viewed as important or unique

- Tends to be self-critical or reactively blames, devalues, and manipulates others

In relationships, a white knight tends to show many of the following behaviors:

- Is attracted to a needy partner or a partner with a history of trauma, loss, abuse, or addiction

- Fears being separated from the partner, losing the partner's love or approval, or being abandoned by the partner

- Engages in controlling behavior, often under the guise of helping

- Maintains or restores connection with the partner by being extremely helpful or good

- Responds ambivalently to the partner's success

- Describes a sense of "oneness" with the partner

- Fails to recognize the partner's manipulative behaviors

- Is seduced by the sexual or dramatic behavior of the partner

- Evokes strong feelings in the partner in order to avoid his or her own emotional discomfort

- Maintains hope for a gratifying relationship by denying the reality of the partner's issues

The Subtypes

To create our subtypes we reviewed numerous cases of rescuing behavior in intimate relationships. We examined and compared the personality styles, behavior in relationships, and early history. From this review, four basic subtypes of rescuers emerged: the overly empathic white knight, the tarnished white knight, the terrorizing/terrified white knight, and the balanced rescuer. These subtypes are not discrete entities but represent our observation of clusters of characteristics that can overlap. Within these subtypes we have noted certain dominant psychological qualities. But these qualities are not necessarily fixed or permanent. Some white knights, for example, move from one subtype to another as they gain insight and perspective from experiences, situations, or major changes in their lives.

The Overly Empathic White Knight

The overly empathic white knight fears emotional distance. This fear can be triggered by many sources, such as separation, loss of love, or loss of approval.

She tries to maintain or restore an emotional connection to her partner by being needed, good, or caregiving and by positively affecting her partner's emotions. Sexual jealousy and insecurity can trigger her fear of emotional distance. As a result, the overly empathic white knight is driven to further prove that she is a valued partner and lover.

The overly empathic white knight worries excessively about her partner. This worry is especially apparent during separations or when she feels he needs her help or protection, lest he experience some kind of discomfort. One overly empathetic white knight worried that her partner had not planned his work schedule properly and that his poor planning might cause him to experience too much stress. Although she may have been correct in predicting her partner's stress, when she created a computer spreadsheet for his various tasks to help him better manage his time, he resented her help and felt humiliated. In situations like these, the white knight often feels hurt, if not angry, when her partner rebuffs her offerings, or perceives her help as a criticism or a nuisance.

As with most white knights, the overly empathic white knight may privately take some of the credit for his partner's success. Yet he may also view his partner's success with ambivalence. Because this white knight fears emotional distance, he may worry that if his partner is successful, she may no longer need the relationship or want it to continue. The major psychological forces at work within this white knight are a heightened sense of empathy, excessive guilt, and an intense fear of emotional distance. These forces are manifested in a variety of ways.

■ Sara

Thirty-one-year-old Sara began therapy after she ended her one-year relationship with her boyfriend, Peter. Sara was a financial consultant whose professional success stood in stark contrast to the poverty of her childhood. When Sara was eleven, her alcoholic father lost his job, and because of his intermittent bingeing, he was able to find only menial employment from which he was repeatedly fired. This financial hardship required Sara's mother to work overtime, leaving Sara responsible for maintaining the home and caring for her two younger brothers. In spite of these burdens, Sara did well in school and won a college scholarship. She left for college but always felt guilty for doing so.

Looking back at her college years, Sara realized that all of her boyfriends had been marginal students whom she had propped up. She'd help them with their term papers, do their laundry, and on one occasion she paid her boyfriend's overdue credit card bill. This pattern continued in her postcollegiate life. As a financial consultant, she mentored others on a regular basis. She met Peter when she was a consultant to his division of a small company.

The disorganization and financial chaos Sara found in Peter's work environment was echoed in his life outside of work. His home was a wreck, his financial situation a mess, and his job status at the company very uncertain. Sara got his division and his life organized. As they grew closer, Peter relinquished most of his responsibilities to her, saying that she was just better and quicker at them than he was. Although Sara liked being helpful and loved how much Peter needed and appreciated her, she slowly became resentful.

When Sara came down with mononucleosis and was exhausted for several weeks, Peter's helplessness and unwillingness to support her became intolerable. Feeling too guilty to leave the relationship, Sara told him that she wanted a trial separation. Peter promised he would change, insisting that it was unfair for her to leave and that he could not survive without her. Peter's pleadings played right into Sara's childhood guilt, and reluctantly, she gave him another chance. But when he soon reverted to his typical helplessness, Sara again asked him to leave. This time, Peter flew into a rage and yelled, "You'll never find anyone else who will love you the way I do."

Now, Sara was teary and unable to sleep. She was terrified that she had made a mistake by ending the relationship and feared that she would always be alone.

Sara is an example of an overly empathic white knight, groomed since childhood to be a rescuer. Carrying so much responsibility in her childhood made Sara feel powerful, but it also gave her the message that her own needs were secondary to the needs of others—and, in fact, they were. Her parents' financial troubles and her mother's need to work long hours had required Sara to give up much of the freedom of childhood in order to help her family. Although leaving home had provided Sara with a college education and a successful career, her guilt about leaving remained. She continually sought out relationships where her guilt would be appeased and where she could be the rescuer that she herself had needed. Peter had recognized Sara's vulnerabilities and then used them to hurt her by saying aloud what she silently feared—that she would never be loved again.

The Tarnished White Knight

The tarnished white knight wants to be loved and appreciated. He seeks to compensate for, and repair, the ineffectual sense of self that he developed in childhood. When this white knight was a child, he may have teased or shamed his peers in order to disguise his self-contempt. When he is in a relationship in which he is adored and idealized, the tarnished white knight feels powerful and potent. He behaves in ways that disguise his vulnerability, fear of abandonment, and feelings of shame and inadequacy. Seeing himself as sexually powerful and skillful is extremely important to the tarnished white knight. Glamorizing his partner and eroticizing their relationship enables him to glorify himself. Sometimes this white knight's need for validation is greater than his partner can provide, which frequently leads him to have affairs outside of his partnership.

The tarnished white knight often chooses partners who have some trait that, by ordinary standards, creates a tangible disparity between herself and her partner. Appearance, health, social, or economic status are common examples of traits that create such disparities. At other times, she has an unrealistic or inflated sense of who her partner is or should be (that is, she exaggerates her partner's talents).

Whatever the disparity, the tarnished white knight's main goal in relationships is to be loved and admired, and he will go to great lengths to achieve that admiration in an effort to heal his past. Unfortunately, this kind of healing rarely works, because the tarnished white knight has an emotional hole within himself that cannot contain whatever new love and admiration is given to him, thus leaving him perpetually needy and frustrated.

▪ Tom

Thirty-three-year-old Tom came for therapy after Nicole, his wife of four years, filed for divorce, stating that Tom was "too needy." Tom had heard this criticism from other women before, and he'd decided to seek help in understanding his partners' reactions to him.

Tom had an unspecified learning disability that had set him apart from his intellectual biochemist parents and his two high-achieving older brothers. When Tom was a child his father had spent countless hours drilling him on facts and concepts, and then screaming at him when Tom could not absorb the lesson, while his mother yelled from another room, "Stop it. You know Tom can't do that!" Eventually, his father gave up, calling Tom "an embarrassment." Tom's mother had often humiliated him further by publicly criticizing his teachers or arranging for his special classes in an abrasive manner.

In middle school, Tom discovered sports, where he excelled in several arenas. This gave him a high status among his fellow students and accolades from his older brothers. His parents, however, thought that sports were a waste of time, and they attended Tom's games only when pressured by his brothers. Because of Tom's skills as an athlete, he was accepted at a local college, where he completed a degree in physical therapy. He then was hired at a clinic several hours away from his hometown. Tom joined the county's baseball and soccer teams, and quickly became a local hero.

Most of the women Tom dated were physical therapy patients at the clinic where he worked. Often his girlfriends were athletes and, when their injuries had healed, Tom wanted to attend their practices and provide additional coaching, which the women found controlling and stifling. His complaints, criticisms, and inability to let them lead their own lives eventually led to the dissolution of the relationship.

Tom met Nicole at a party. She had been in an accident that had left her with severe knee pain. Because of her pain, getting out of a chair was sometimes difficult for her. Tom had noticed her struggling and had discreetly come to her aid. They dated for six months and then married. Nicole, an administrative assistant at a local newspaper, was proud that her husband was such a stellar athlete, and she spoke to her editor about writing a weekly column on the local sports teams. The editor agreed, and Nicole's column became a hit.

Nicole's new job required her presence at many games, not just those in which Tom played, and Tom began to resent the attention the other games demanded from her. As a result, he became overtly critical of her and made derogatory comments about her column. One day, Nicole showed up unexpectedly after one of Tom's games and found him flirting with and kissing a fan. He told Nicole that this behavior was due to her lack of attention to him and her disregard for what he found important. After a number of quarrels about these issues, Nicole filed for divorce.

In childhood, Tom's learning disability, together with his parents' self-centered responses to that disability, had significantly contributed to Tom's sense of shame. His father's dismissal of him as an "embarrassment" and his mother's well-meaning but clumsy intrusions had confirmed Tom's feelings of inadequacy and taught him to blame others for his difficulties.

Tom's tendency to have relationships with women needing physical therapy represented his wish to be in control, needed, and admired. But Nicole had her own agenda, which at times took precedence over Tom's. Tom's fragile sense of self, self-centeredness, and shame made his perception of being second in Nicole's life intolerable, and caused him to treat her in the same manner as his father had treated him—with criticism and humiliation.

The Terrorizing/Terrified White Knight

The terrorizing/terrified white knight is the subtype most likely to have experienced overwhelming fear and shame as a child. This white knight tends to have had a very traumatic early childhood that may have included sexual, emotional, or physical abuse. Such an extremely difficult childhood has left her with limited skills to handle her psychological burden.

The terrorizing/terrified white knight learned to be highly manipulative of her parents, teachers, and peers as an adaptation and reaction to her childhood experiences. She may have been deceitful, a bully, and most likely believed that she was entitled to special treatment—all of which served temporarily to counteract her shame and fear by making her feel, in the moment, powerful and special. The remnants of this unhealthy coping style can be seen in her adult personality. This white knight copes by creating situations where others feel afraid or shamed.

Through various behaviors, the terrorizing/terrified white knight transfers her feelings of emptiness, jealousy, shame, anger, and fear of abandonment to her partner. She may be accusatory, critical, or mocking in an attempt to relieve herself of shame by shaming him. The terrorizing/terrified white knight often uses sex and jealousy to control her partner.

■ Lexie

Twenty-five-year-old Lexie came to therapy as a condition imposed by a court order. Her frequent loud, disruptive, and physical fights with her boyfriend, Jason, had led to the destruction of property and injuries to him. Lexie had shown no embarrassment when she admitted the truth of the accusations, but she justified her actions by saying, "I wasn't going to just sit there and take it."

Lexie's mother had been a prostitute who had supported Lexie, her pimp boyfriend, and herself with her earnings. Because Lexie's mother was a drug addict and was often incapacitated, Lexie had been left completely unprotected from sexual and physical assaults by her mother's boyfriend. When Lexie was eight years old, she'd told her mother about the boyfriend's assaults. Her mother had confronted her boyfriend, who'd responded by punching Lexie's mother, knocking her out, and giving her a concussion.

When she saw her mother unconscious, Lexie had become so frightened that she promised herself she would never complain about anything to her mother again. Several months later, a teacher had noticed bruises on Lexie's arms and legs, and filed a report with a child protective services agency. Ultimately, the social service agency removed Lexie from her mother's home and placed her in foster care with her mother's cousin, a bookkeeper in a nearby town. Shortly after, Lexie's mother died of a drug overdose, for which Lexie blamed her mother's boyfriend.

Although her mother's cousin had provided a loving home, throughout elementary and junior high school, Lexie was frequently suspended for fighting, using profanity, and cruel teasing. At sixteen, she'd joined a gang, whose main activities centered around drug abuse and car theft. When she was seventeen, she'd contracted gonorrhea but had ignored the symptoms until the disease had progressed and caused infertility.

Lexie had started a car-detailing business with her mother's cousin's help, and for a short period of time she stayed away from her gang associates, gave up using drugs, and became celibate. But after her mother's cousin died, Lexie had resumed both her drug use and promiscuous behavior.

Lexie met Jason when she literally rescued him from the roadside. He was staring at his car's engine, totally lost, bewildered, and overwhelmed when Lexie drove by. She stopped to help and quickly got the engine running. Jason, twenty-two, worked at a local grocery store. His parents were active "swingers," and throughout his childhood they had callously teased him for being embarrassed by their flagrant sexual behavior. As a result, he'd had few sexual experiences and had become addicted to Internet pornography. Lexie became his literal idol, someone who could do or handle anything. She thought Jason was "as cute as a puppy" and enjoyed introducing him to sexuality and various recreational drugs. They soon moved in together.

At first things went well. Lexie found Jason's sexual inexperience exciting and she enjoyed "being on top," but as time went by, she became frustrated by his passivity. She thought he was allowing his supervisor to "push him around," and would rage at him for coming home late from work. Once, she put his job in jeopardy by calling the supervisor about changing his work schedule. And she vehemently objected to spending any money for food, believing that Jason should "just take it" from the store. Jason crumbled at her criticism and retreated to pornography, which made Lexie feel ignored, hurt, and angry. She responded by viciously insulting him, provoking him to respond. Invariably, their quarrels would end with the neighbors or Jason calling the police.

Given Lexie's traumatic background, it is not surprising that she developed such a tough exterior. As a child, she'd handled her terror by bullying and terrifying other children. She also carried a burden of tremendous guilt and shame that she had caused her mother to be injured by revealing the sexual abuse that she had endured; she had not hidden her bruises, which caused her removal from her home, and had left her mother alone and unprotected. As an adolescent, she'd found solace and friendship with other terrified adolescents, who in turn, had terrified others.

Lexie found another fearful person in Jason, but rather than being aggressive, Jason's fears had pushed him inward. Although she had helped him to feel sexual and become more assertive, ultimately, the consequences of Jason's early life experiences were beyond Lexie's ability to help. In order to cope with Jason's withdrawal and her own sense of helplessness, she responded much as she had throughout her life, by turning her fear into anger and rage.

The Balanced Rescuer

The balanced rescuer is sensitive to the needs of others and practices altruism for its own sake. He gives support freely and is not conflicted about his partner's success. These are healthy, generous men and women who are respected by others. Having found a partner who carries her own weight, the balanced rescuer will anticipate reciprocity in his relationships. He and his partner are willing to support each other through the good times and bad. He helps when asked, but also offers help freely and graciously, without implying criticism or trying to control. While white knights may feel threatened when things go well for their partners, the balanced rescuer is truly delighted. Although he may quietly take some pride in whatever help he has provided, he goes out of his way to ensure that his partner receives the credit for her successes.

▪ Greg

Greg, a forty-three-year-old hospital administrator, came for a consultation with Linda, his wife of twelve years. Both Greg and Linda, but especially Greg, sought guidance in dealing with their children around the issue of Linda's upcoming treatment for uterine cancer.

When Greg was six years old, his mother had been diagnosed with lymphoma. Since the most innovative treatment was available only in a city four hours away from the family's dairy business and home, his mother had moved to the city for her year-long treatment. Every three weeks, Greg, his eight-year-old sister, and their father visited Greg's mother. Frightened by how sick his mother had looked at their first visit, Greg had not wanted to return. But his father had insisted that Greg should continue visiting his mother, reminding him of how sad she would be if he didn't.

Greg's mother had been a fighter who completed her treatment and then resumed her life at home. During Greg's teenage years, his father turned to alcohol, often musing about "unfulfilled dreams" and falling asleep in front of the television set. Greg's mother developed a surprising interest in the stock market, and she wisely invested the dairy's meager profits, which put both of her children through college.

Shortly after Greg completed his degree in public health, his father died. Greg reacted to his father's death by becoming a problem drinker. When he received a DUI (driving under the influence) citation, he decided to quit drinking and focus on his career. He then met Linda, who had a good job, friends, and savings but had not yet found Mr. Right.

"Greg," she said, "rescued me from spinsterhood," a statement Greg quickly dismissed. He described Linda then and now as "strong, capable, and having good values." They married, had two daughters, and were doing well. They'd developed a way to talk through their differences or just to let them go. Linda felt that Greg pampered her: "If it's raining but I've got a cookie craving, he'll go out and get cookies." Greg felt that Linda was a great companion who added both fun and stability to his life. Their sex life waxed and waned, but neither felt rejected when the other wasn't interested.

When Linda became ill, Greg continued to be helpful and supportive. He researched the Internet about her disease, used his connections at the hospital to investigate treatment options, and rescheduled his work and business travel so that he could go with her to her medical appointments. Although he was distraught about her illness, he said that it was his job to keep things positive and moving forward, and that if he allowed himself to ruminate on the more frightening thoughts, he would be less able to help. He added that Linda was "holding it together really well."

Greg was a balanced rescuer. He had chosen a good partner, friend, coparent, and lover. Even though Linda's diagnosis threw Greg's life far out of balance, he rose to the occasion by making his business affairs secondary to being present and supportive for his wife during her treatment. Then, demonstrating empathy based on his own painful childhood memories and uncertainty during his mother's absence and illness, Greg sought consultation to help his daughters.

Although Greg was a balanced rescuer, his childhood had been far from perfect, and he had suffered the trauma of the temporary loss of his mother and seeing her so ill. However, his father's stable presence and his mother's fighting spirit communicated to Greg that his parents were strong and, by extension, that Greg was safe. His father's response to Greg's hesitation to visit his mother had made Greg feel guilty, but it also communicated that Greg was strong enough to handle visiting his mother and that, at times, it was necessary to put his own fears aside in order to help someone else. This is what Greg was now doing as he helped Linda.

After his father's death, Greg's drinking had masked his grief, guilt, and helplessness concerning his father's unhappiness. Through behaving like his father and abusing alcohol, Greg's drinking also served to keep his father symbolically alive and with him. Fortunately, Greg also had identified with the stronger father of his early childhood, as well as with his "fighter" mother. Recognizing the dangerous path he was on, Greg successfully changed course: he stopped drinking and established a meaningful relationship.

Temporary White Knights

A temporary white knight is someone who has been in high-functioning relationships but with the onset of some unusual stressors, such as the loss of a job or the illness or death of someone close, pursues an unhealthy rescuing relationship. Our use of the term "white knight syndrome" implies a chronic need to be the rescuer in intimate relationships. Temporary white knights do not demonstrate chronic rescuing and, technically, do not fall into our sub-types. However, we have seen a number of people who temporarily rescue in an unhealthy manner, and we illustrate one such case below, although we will not discuss this subtype elsewhere in the book.

■ Janice

Janice came to therapy confused by her eight-month-long extra-marital affair with her guitar teacher, Adam. Although she had been happily married to Jim for twenty-five years, she now believed that with Adam she had found "communication and true sharing." Janice's early history included the trauma of discovering her six-month-old sister lifeless in her crib when Janice was five years old. Subsequently, Janice's mother suffered a severe depression that required several hos-pitalizations. Because of her mother's physical and emotional absence from the home, Janice's nurturing paternal grandmother moved in with them. Her grandmother remained in the family home until she died, when Janice was in college.

Even with this difficult history, Janice had created a good mar-riage, and she described Jim as "a loving father and husband." They enjoyed similar activities, had two healthy sons, and treated each other with courtesy and respect. Janice was also an active member of her community and had developed educational and cultural pro-grams for the school system.

Shortly before her fiftieth birthday, Janice experienced a series of stressors: her youngest son left for college; her father broke his hip but refused to move into an assisted-living situation; and Janice lost in a local school board election, which left her feeling betrayed by her community and wondering if she had done something wrong. It was during this period that Janice began her affair with Adam.

Adam had a history of at least one psychiatric hospitalization, struggled with recreational drug use, and often needed to borrow money to cover his rent. Janice recognized that Adam was unstable, and she knew that it would be foolish of her to give up all she had for someone like him. But Adam made her feel alive, and that feeling was addicting. She had tried to end the relationship several times and have just a platonic friendship with him, but that had never lasted. She hoped that therapy would help her to understand her own behav-ior and her "addiction," as well as help her discover a way to end the relationship.

Janice's early childhood contained significant losses, guilt, and shame. Although as an adult she intellectually understood that she was not responsible either for her sister's death or her mother's depression, as a child she had felt responsible, as children often do. Emotionally stabilized by her paternal grandmother's presence, she had married Jim and created a happy and fulfilled life. Indeed, one might question whether Janice would have become involved with Adam had it not been for this particular combination of stressors, which may have symbolically represented her childhood traumas.

The community's rejection of Janice for the school board position triggered her childhood feelings of shame and helplessness. Although, in reality, her son's departure for college represented her successful parenting, this reality was overshadowed by memories of her sister's death and the accompanying sense of guilt. The additional stress of taking care of her father may have triggered her childhood feelings of being powerless when she had tried to make her depressed mother happy. The thoughts about mortality that a fiftieth birthday can cause must have only added to her overtaxed psychological state. The illicit quality of her affair with Adam provided excitement and danger that took her away from her current troubles. His obvious pathology, which paralleled her mother's, provided Janice with the opportunity to rescue, to have the power to successfully "fix" someone in the present, where she had been unsuccessful in childhood.

The Rescuer Who May Also Be the Rescued

Now that we have delineated the character traits of white knights, we want to note that sometimes the demarcation between the white knight and the rescued partner can be obscured. At times, we have found that if we look deeper into the dynamics of the relationship, the person who appears to be the one being rescued is, in fact, the one doing the rescuing; and the apparent rescuer is the person being rescued.

We will be focusing on the partner who is predominantly the white knight in the relationship. You may find that both the role of the white knight and the role of the person being rescued may resonate with you. We discuss the interchangeable roles of the white knight and the rescued person more thoroughly in chapter 8.

The White Knight Syndrome

It is the obvious mark of a healthy relationship when each partner supports and helps the other in both good times and bad. The difference between the balanced rescuer and the white knight relationship is that in the balanced, healthy relationship, the helping partner, at both a conscious and an unconscious level, is helping out of love and concern.

When we refer to the white knight syndrome, we are referring to the unhealthy behavior of the overly empathic, tarnished, or terrorizing/terrified white knight. The self-esteem of the white knight depends on other people's recognition of his heroic qualities. This paradigm, in which the white knight's self-esteem is linked to another's weakness, means that he can feel good about himself only when he anticipates providing relief, pleasure, or happiness to someone who has a need that he can fulfill. With his self-esteem contingent on another's weakness rather than on a secure and healthy sense of self, the white knight's self-esteem will always be in jeopardy and his relationships will be dysfunctional.

The white knight syndrome results from an individual's efforts to repair her damaged sense of self by rescuing a partner who will, in turn, nurture and idealize her. The white knight wants to safely experience her passion, sensitivity, and vulnerability. Sadly and self-destructively, safety for the white knight can be found only with partners who seemingly have less power than her own. Thus, her choice of a partner and how she eventually treats that partner not only prevent her from moving beyond the damage inflicted on her self-esteem in her childhood, they also repeat that damage. Not surprisingly, white knights often end up feeling shamed and humiliated instead of gaining the sense of power they had hoped to achieve. In chapter 2, "The White Knight in Training," you will learn more about the white knight's childhood and how it contributes to her chronic need to rescue others.

Thinking About It

Now, take a look at your answers to the questionnaire that appeared at the end of the introduction. That questionnaire was created to provide you with a guideline for reviewing your behavior and experience. If most or all of your answers match the answers shown below, there is a very good chance that you are suffering from the white knight syndrome.

Answers to the Questionnaire, Are You a White Knight?

1. *My partner made me feel idolized in the beginning of our relationship.*

    True. The white knight wants to be idolized or admired even if the qualities for which he is adored are unrealistic or inflated. Balanced rescuers want to be loved, cherished, and appreciated by their partners for who they really are.

2. *I have to be extremely watchful of what I say or do, lest I upset or anger my partner.*

    True. The overly empathic, tarnished, or terrorizing/terrified white knights are often in relationships with people who have little control over their emotions—what therapists describe as being "emotionally volatile." Many times, when the partner does lose control, the white knight becomes the focus of a partner's rage or feels guilty about the partner's despair. Thus, although white knights may think that they are in control, they are really under the control of their partners. The balanced rescuer trusts his partner to handle her difficult emotions appropriately, which gives him the freedom to communicate with her honestly.

3. *I feel that the responsibility of managing my life, together with my partner's, all rests upon me.*

    True. Some white knights would acknowledge that their partners do manage some of the less important areas of the relationship. However, most white knights feel, and perhaps unconsciously desire, that their partners could not manage without them. Balanced rescuers see life with their partners as a cooperative venture with a give-and-take that involves them both.

4. *I have stayed in relationships out of a sense of guilt or worry about my partner.*

    True. Many white knights have such a strong sense of empathy that they cannot bear thinking they might be the cause of their partners' pain. Other white knights feel needed to such a degree that they truly fear their partners could not survive without them. Balanced rescuers realize that for a relationship to succeed, they and their partners must be happy, and that staying in a relationship out of guilt or fear would be a disservice to both of them. Most importantly, the balanced rescuer has the inner strength to tolerate being the short-term cause of his partner's pain, if the anticipated long-term result is positive.

5. *At the start of the relationship, I saw my partner as dangerously exciting or exotic.*

    True. White knights avoid looking at themselves and their own unhappiness by being in an uncertain, precarious situation that forces their attention outward, as opposed to inward. Thus, they will choose unstable partners whose instability provides a distraction, over stable partners whose stability creates a calm that allows unpleasant feelings to come forward. The balanced rescuer seeks out a calm and stable partner, recognizing the freedom that having such a strong foundation provides.

6. *Often, I know better than my partner what is best for him or her.*

    True. White knights need to be needed and often inflate their understanding of their partners' needs. Balanced rescuers maintain a realistic view of their own and their partners' strengths and weaknesses. They choose partners who are self-aware and have good judgment. As a result, they can trust their partners to make healthy and informed decisions.

7. *People don't realize that I am extremely self-critical.*

    True. White knights are plagued by feelings of self-criticism or self-contempt, which they feel as guilt or shame. Sometimes white knights will avoid these feelings by manipulating, devaluing, and blaming their partners. Balanced rescuers forgive themselves and others for their imperfections and mistakes.

8. *I often disregard my own needs to focus on just my partner's needs.*

    True. White knights consider themselves to be altruists or self-sacrificing partners. Often, however, their altruistic acts are attempts to feel powerful, or needed, or to cover a sense of guilt or shame. Balanced rescuers help their partners out of genuine concern and caring.

9. *I often feel that my partner doesn't appreciate all that I do for him or her.*

   True. Whether or not the partner is appreciative, white knights rarely feel that their partners fully appreciate them. White knights typically feel unappreciated, because they seek a response that their partners can't provide: a healing of their past hurts and relief from their sense of being defective, flawed, or unworthy. Since balanced rescuers have a healthy sense of self, the level of appreciation they seek is attainable.

10. *I look back on many of my relationships and realize I have been rescuing my partners.*

   True. Repeatedly finding partners in need of rescue is the defining trait of a white knight. Consciously or unconsciously, white knights are attracted to others who need rescuing. Balanced rescuers want to be helpful to their partners but do not repeatedly seek out, nor are they inherently attracted to, partners who need rescuing.

2

The White Knight
in Training

You became who you are through your relationships with caregivers, siblings, peers, and mentors. Biological predispositions, sociocultural factors, and an array of experiences influenced how you think about yourself and how you interact with others. In this chapter, we explore how childhood relationships, experiences, and predispositions contribute to the development of the white knight syndrome. Many of the concepts we present here—including altruism, empathy, guilt, shame, and narcissistic features—will be discussed in greater detail in later chapters.

■ Andrew

Andrew is a young boy who has developed the self-defeating, rescuing behavior we find in the white knight syndrome. He was a psychotherapy patient for brief, intermittent periods of time from the ages of eight to fourteen. Andrew's parents divorced when he was seven years old. His mother, a beautiful, seductive, self-centered, and emotionally unstable woman, wished for a "freer life," and relinquished custody to Andrew's father, who, fortunately, was a loving and nurturing parent.

After the divorce, Andrew's mother visited Andrew sporadically and occasionally had him stay with her for a few days. During these visits she treated him as a confidant, keeping him up late into the night telling him about her troubles with the men she dated. Not surprisingly, her relationships with men were filled with drama. As a result, her mood was either very happy or very depressed, yet whenever Andrew visited her, he thought she was perfect. He became her admirer, friend, and the defender who always took his mother's side during her arguments with his father.

When Andrew was eight years old, he'd told his therapist that he wished he could be Superman, a role he frequently enacted during his therapy sessions. As an adolescent, when he was seen in treatment again, Andrew had grown into his own version of a superhero, repeatedly taking care of unhappy or troubled girls. In one instance, he'd become very involved with a depressed and suicidal female classmate. Feeling responsible for this girl's welfare, Andrew often called her, her parents, or the school counselor to make sure she was safe. His concern for others and his inclination to rescue them was at the expense of his own academic, emotional, and social life.

Andrew's father, a white knight himself, had originally become involved with Andrew's mother for similar reasons: he had wanted to save her from her self-destructive behavior, and he had believed his stability would provide her with the security she had wanted. At the same time, he was drawn to her high energy and dramatic neediness. After the divorce, through psychotherapy and increasing self-awareness, he was eventually able to establish a relationship with a woman that was mutually nurturing and satisfying. As a result of better understanding himself, he was able to recognize his son's conflicts and needs.

Attachment and Your Brain

Whatever it is that attracts one person to another may be something that cannot be articulated; thus, we call it "chemistry." But this simple chemical explanation of what attracts one person to another has been found to have an actual, complex neurobiological basis, a capacity that exists within the human brain at birth (Fisher 2006).

The relationships you had with your childhood caregivers became embedded in your mind as *implicit memories.* Implicit memories are outside of your awareness and can influence your preferences in partners. So the inclination to become a white knight, or to have one as a partner, is not necessarily determined consciously. Some theorists speculate that buried in our minds are qualities or images that resonate with certain people we meet, which can create a feeling of attraction. These attractors are patterns that are more or less imprinted on the *limbic system* of the brain, generally thought to be the center of emotions (Lewis, Amini, and Lannon 2000).

Researchers have recognized and studied the ways in which children read their caregivers' facial expressions, display emotions on their own faces before being conscious of specific feelings, and mirror facial expressions that become experienced internally as emotions (Ekman 1972; Izard 1971). The ability to send emotional signals to your caregivers and receive such signals from them forms the basis of early attachment (Flores 2004; Meltzoff and Moore 1977). The basic mechanisms for imitative learning, as well as for the development of attachment and empathy, are innately present in your brain. These mechanisms are important to the child's developing capacity to form relationships with others. They also affect the quality of those relationships, including the potential to develop white knight behavior.

Relationships Create Beliefs

Early in your life, you may have developed unhealthy patterns in order to obtain the emotional connections you needed. Often, such unhealthy patterns persist into adulthood and predispose you to have certain kinds of relationships. During your childhood, as you adapted to your experiences with your caregivers, you developed certain beliefs about yourself and others. Generally, the beliefs that children develop are healthy and move them toward forming positive relationships and purposeful lives. For example, a secure relationship with your parents may have led you to assume that you can trust others to care about your needs. At other times, the beliefs that are developed can detrimentally affect how the child feels about herself and prevent her from pursuing or achieving her desired goals.

Pathogenic Beliefs

Unhealthy beliefs that children develop about themselves and their care-givers that interfere with their self-esteem and social functioning are described as *pathogenic* (Weiss 1993). Andrew, for example, developed the pathogenic belief that he was responsible for his mother's well-being, which later extended to his overly responsible behavior toward others. This belief also led him to assume that he wielded awesome powers of authority and control, which con-trasted sharply with his buried feelings of being weak, ineffectual, and unable to help his mother. Being consciously aware of his own weakness and his disap-pointment in his mother would have been too overwhelming and frightening for Andrew. Adapting to his reality, he needed to protect his mother and his image of her, thus shielding himself from his feelings of helplessness, abandon-ment, and disappointment in her.

Although pathogenic beliefs can cause much suffering in your life, when they are played out repeatedly in later relationships, their purpose, in part, has to do with remaining loyal to the early relationships that created them. In Andrew's case, loyalty to his mother maintained his belief that she was perfect.

Research conducted by Joseph Weiss (1993) demonstrated that people have an unconscious plan that motivates them toward achieving healthy behavior. So in spite of this loyalty to early relationship patterns, throughout your life you are also highly motivated to disprove and alter those beliefs and to overcome unhealthy patterns, regardless of how rigid or repetitive those beliefs and patterns may appear to be.

Attachment Theory

Attachment theory provides us with an understanding of how our early relationships with caregivers influence the ways in which we interact with others, and whom we choose as partners. According to *attachment theory*, the child uses her experiences with caregivers as models for what she should expect from others. Through these experiences she forms beliefs about herself in her relationships (Bowlby 1982).

If a child's parents or caregivers were consistently and lovingly available to her, she is more likely to feel secure and confident in her adult relationships. On the other hand, if her caregivers were self-centered, negligent, unpredict-able, intimidating, overprotective, or unavailable, she is more likely to feel insecure, helpless, and unworthy of forming satisfying adult relationships. She may try to cope with her helplessness and deep insecurity with needy, dependent, or clingy behavior, or she may protect herself by distancing from relationships, using behavior that is self-centered, arrogant, or perfectionistic (Horney 1950).

These responses can later appear in the adult white knight personality as *narcissistic features*, such as an excessive need for admiration and an overestimation of one's abilities and appearance. However, keep in mind that these personality traits are an adaptation to caregivers and circumstances that did not offer what was needed for the child's healthy development. Even self-centeredness, which you might regard in a negative way, can be understood as an attempt to later give yourself what you did not receive (Flores 2004).

Little Rescuers

Altruism and empathy develop early in life and play an important role in white knight behavior. These qualities are observed in children who are sensitive to the needs of others. But being an altruistic and empathic child also has a downside.

Childhood Altruism

Why is it that some children have a strong inclination toward helping behavior, yet others do not? Six-year-old Anna was described by her teacher as a child who always sought out "loners and kids who needed help." If a classmate was in need, Anna was certain to recognize it and try to assist. In contrast, eight-year-old Katie limited her friendships at school to kids who were part of the popular crowd, and she ignored the children who were not admired. Yet another child, Ella, constantly offered to help her classmates with their homework, hoping they would become her friends and invite her to sit with them at lunch. When Ella's help failed to obtain a spot for her at the classmate's lunch table, she became resentful and withdrawn.

Nancy McWilliams (1984) describes how early-childhood loss, trauma, or disappointment, along with a rescuing or inspiring role model, has been found in the histories of adults who tend to be altruistic. She adds, however, that not all adults who suffered loss, trauma, or disappointment as children will develop altruistic tendencies; those who have experienced being "rescued" themselves may be most inclined to become altruistic adults.

The altruistic tendencies and empathic capacity that you develop as a child may be linked to the style of parenting you received. Martin Hoffman (2000) believes that when a parent uses *power-assertive discipline,* which employs physical punishment and the withholding of privileges, or *withdrawal of love discipline,* which employs withdrawing parental affection or approval, the child's focus will be on what the child will lose, as opposed to focusing on the impact of her behavior.

Suppose Ariel hits her younger sister, and her mother responds by giving Ariel a time-out and sending Ariel to her room, saying that she doesn't want to be around her for a while. Ariel's focus will now be on the loss of her mother's affection and the loss of her opportunity to play. On the other hand, if a parent focuses the child's attention on the impact of the child's actions on other people, the child will develop an internal motive to consider others that is empathy-based (Hoffman 2000).

In our example, if Ariel's mother would talk to Ariel about how she has made her sister feel, Ariel may become aware of the effect of her behavior on her sister's feelings. This will help her to develop empathy and the ability to see things from another person's perspective. If her mother's response focuses Ariel's attention exclusively on what Ariel is losing (her mother's affection and the opportunity to continue playing), that does nothing to help Ariel develop an internal motive for becoming empathic toward her sister.

Hoffman believes that empathy-focused parental responses foster the development of a morality that can override self-serving motivations and lead to altruistic behavior. In chapter 3 we will review some of the theories and research concerning altruism and examine how these relate to white knight rescuing behavior.

The Perils of Childhood Empathy

The capacity for *empathy,* that is, experiencing or knowing what another person is feeling by seeing oneself in the other, is an essential interpersonal skill. But empathy can also lead to guilt, anxiety, and distress in children. This may occur because a child's ability to perceive feelings in another may develop long before his ability to interpret these feelings appropriately. The sensitivity of the child, coupled with his maintaining a constant inner awareness of the emotional state of his caregivers, can lead him to believe he is responsible for his caregivers' feelings in both positive and negative ways.

For example, a twelve year old boy who was a budding overly empathic white knight heard numerous stories about how his mother had been emotionally and physically hurt by her abusive father. He then felt that it was his calling to challenge bullies, and he fought numerous fights, often at the expense of his own broken bones, in the name of honor and justice.

Because of their heightened awareness, empathic children want to please their caregivers. They believe that a parent's mood is dependent on their behavior. If they are good, their mother is happy. If they are entertaining or clever, their father's mood is pleasant, and his self-esteem as a parent is affected in a positive way. Conversely, if a parent is unhappy, the child may assume responsibility by blaming herself and her behavior for her parent's unhappiness. Such interactions happen unconsciously for the most part. Nonetheless, imagine the strain on a child who must anxiously attend to her parents' emotions, especially if she feels guilty and responsible for failing to positively influence her parents' moods.

Even in the best of homes, the child will experience events and situations that challenge his self-esteem and create anxiety and guilt. Yet a sensitive and vulnerable child, one who has a depressed or self-absorbed parent, a child who has endured some form of trauma, or one who lives in a heightened state of anxiety may have an exaggerated belief about the effects of his behavior on the happiness of others. At the same time, a child may fear his own feelings of help-lessness or feel ashamed and inadequate when he is powerless.

■ Jon: An Empathic Rescuer

Seven-year-old Jon sat at a table with his therapist. Without any prompting he drew a picture of a tall, narrow castle surrounded by a moat. A large, wooden drawbridge in the up position served as the front door. Jon carefully added a window near the top of the castle with a figure peering out. He identified the figure as the therapist, who needed to be rescued from the dragon. Jon saved her from the dragon by drawing himself and the therapist flying away from the castle. He then reassured the therapist that he "slayed the dragon" and that now she is safe.

Depending on the child's age and psychological development, children in psychotherapy often work on their problems indirectly through their play and drawings. Sometimes they use the therapist to symbolically represent an important person in their lives. When Jon drew his picture, he was most likely communicating his fears about his own and his mother's safety.

Jon's fears are quite reasonable, given that his father was murdered in a carjacking two years ago. Recently, his mother married a very capable and nurturing man who has provided Jon with a sense of security, as well as being a model of strength and protection with whom Jon can identify. Perhaps this is why he now feels he can be the rescuer and protector he needed for himself and his mother.

Taking the Blame

Because a child is so dependent on her caregivers, she will go to great lengths to maintain her image of them as strong, powerful, and knowledgeable. It is simply too frightening to think otherwise, even if such a distortion involves the unhealthy belief that somehow the child is at fault for the parent's problems or how the parent treats the child.

If a child senses distraction or rejection on the part of his parent or caregiver, he may assume responsibility for that rejection and will seek verification that he is the cause of his parent's behavior. For example, frequently a child will misbehave, which may result in his getting punished, when, in fact, he is assuming responsibility for feelings he perceives in a parent.

Imagine a child watching a parent talking on the telephone and listening to the parent's elevated emotion: the excitement, distress, or concern that is often expressed in a heightened way on the phone. A parent's strong emotion often disturbs children and can be interpreted by them as a sign of parental weakness, fear, impending danger, or emotional separation. As a result, the child may create a commotion that distracts the parent away from her phone conversation and causes her to direct her attention, often angrily, onto her misbehaving child. Unfortunately, this can validate for the child the notion that he is responsible for his parent's feelings.

If a parent is angry and unhappy, the child may perceive the parent's anger and unhappiness as due to the child's inadequacy in order to protect the image of the parent as all-powerful and good. Or if the child is unable to obtain the love and admiration he needs in his relationship with a parent, he may feel inadequate or be vulnerable to shame. When unmet, even normal desires for a parent's love, approval, or attention may be understood by the child in a way that keeps the parent as perfect in the child's mind. Later, in their adult relationships, these children may seek the approval they never received from their parents or caregivers.

Children who are raised in an abusive environment are especially challenged to maintain loyalty to their parents. Judith Herman (1992) suggests that if a child is going to survive in a chronically abusive environment, she must find a way to trust people who are untrustworthy, find safety in an unsafe situation, and exert control in a setting that is unpredictable. In an abusive situation, the child has the impossible task of trying to understand how someone who claims to love her can direct such violence, rage, and hatred at her.

With limited ways to cope, the abused child often has the same emotional reaction of his nonabused counterpart: he understands his parent's behavior by blaming himself. Thus the abused child's identity is formed around a sense of inner badness (Herman 1992). If it is the child who is bad, then the behavior of the parent makes sense and is justified, and his relationship with his parent can remain intact. Although such an understanding may provide short-term relief for the abused child, the long-term consequences can be debilitating.

The long-term effects of child abuse include shame and humiliation. Contrary to a popular fear, a child who is abused does not necessarily become an abuser. Rather, perpetrators of violence often have a history of having been being abused. Thus, the shame and humiliation of having been abused as a child can make one susceptible to violence against oneself or others (Fonagy et al. 2004), but do not inevitably lead one to become an abusive adult.

Shame and Inadequacy

The strong feelings of shame and inadequacy that develop in childhood appear in adult white knight relationships. These feelings may arise from any number of sources, including attachment issues, helplessness, loss, trauma, vulnerability, or a myriad of family circumstances and caregiving behaviors that interfered with the child's sense of security and emotional development.

The Importance of Parental Attunement

One type of caregiving behavior that leads to later problems, including feelings of shame and inadequacy, is called *parental misattunement*. Misattunement occurs when parents are unable to respond appropriately to the child's needs, expectations, and feelings. For example, a child who feels rejected by her peers may be blamed by her parent for her social inadequacies. Similarly, a child may seek the approval of an unresponsive parent because of the parent's own needs.

Parental misattunement can cause a child to develop a readiness or tendency to feel unworthy, flawed, or inferior (Lansky 1994). According to Lansky, attunement failure on the part of primary caregivers can lead to the formation of rigid, inflexible ideals in the child's mind about what and who the child should be, and create frustrating ideals that the child can never achieve. Thus, we can imagine how a child might think that she has to be someone special to attain love, approval, or attention. A child's repeated failure to achieve these ideals can result in feelings of shame and cause the child to become shame-prone. As the child matures, his shame-proneness may lead him to become vulnerable to feeling flawed, different, or depressed (Morrison 1989).

The Many Faces of Childhood Shame

Some shame-prone children can appear shy, inadequate, dependent, or oversensitive, while others may display grandiose and self-centered behavior. In part, the different responses may be the result of whether the child externalizes or internalizes feelings of shame. A child is thought to *externalize* when she disguises her own inner discomfort by believing that it is someone else who is bad or, at the very least, is the cause of her own bad feelings about herself. Externalizing places the source of something you wish to deny outside of yourself. In contrast, some children may *internalize* shame; that is, they attribute the source of the shame to themselves, usually in an exaggerated form, and they view themselves as the bad ones.

Externalizing Feelings of Helplessness, Shame, and Inadequacy

In an effort to disown the shame or weakness they feel within themselves, some budding white knights learn to externalize these feelings by focusing on the shame and weakness in another. For example, a child who feels flawed or different may tease her younger brother ruthlessly, thereby eliciting in him the feeling of inadequacy that previously existed only in herself.

Additionally, making her brother the proxy for her feelings will later give her the opportunity to rescue him by being a source of reassurance. The maneuver of one person finding a proxy in another person for overwhelming feelings that are too uncomfortable to recognize as her own, or of relocating her own feelings onto another is, unfortunately, common in numerous personality disorders and, in different variations, also can be seen in normal individuals (Nathanson 1987; Wangh 1962).

It is not unusual to discover chronic bullying or teasing behavior in the childhood of adults who are prone to shame. If this kind of behavior was typical of your childhood, perhaps you can ask yourself about the source of the shame you were trying to avoid at the time.

Internalizing Feelings of Helplessness, Shame, and Inadequacy

A child will often take on her parents' feelings of shame and weakness by making the shame and weakness her own. This serves to maintain the child's perception of her parents as strong, ideal, and protective. Thus, a parent's shame or weakness can be more easily tolerated if the child believes that she has an equal or greater deficit.

For example, one fifteen-year-old girl internalized her shame and called herself "stupid." Fearing that people would discover her "stupidity," she was shy and withdrawn. Her shyness and withdrawal were really an attempt to make sure that no one ever learned about the abusive, demeaning, and psychotic behavior of her alcoholic mother. By isolating herself and focusing on her own feelings of inadequacy, she hid from herself and others the embarrassment she felt about her mother, and the feelings of helplessness that she experienced.

A child's feelings of helplessness, shame, and inadequacy can further translate into discomfort about his body or anxiety regarding his ability to perform certain tasks. He may not be able to handle the feelings of vulnerability that are held by most children. As a result, a budding white knight may feel weak or compelled to prove himself in a physical or intellectual way. Thus, he relies excessively on the positive opinions of others to feel better about himself. Later, he may constantly seek approval or hide his need by behaving arrogantly, as though he completely disregards what others may think of him.

■ Tyler: A Budding White Knight

Six-year-old Tyler is described as a difficult child by most of the adults in his life. Yet if you look more closely at his behavior, you can see that he is adapting to his circumstances in a desperate way. On the surface, Tyler is constantly misbehaving at school. He hits other children and calls them names. He refuses to do his work, is disrespectful to his teacher and other authority figures, and is often considered out of control. Tyler terrorizes, and at the same time, he is terrified. He behaves as though he is powerful, but he is really trying to hide from himself and others his feeling of being helpless and inadequate.

Tyler's parents are divorced. He lives with his mother during the week and visits his father every other weekend. Tyler's older brother lives primarily with their father. When Tyler is with his father and brother, he claims they "gang up" against him and say "mean things" about him. Although his mother is thirty years old, he refers to her as "a teenager" because "she dresses and acts like a teenager, especially when she goes out on dates." Tyler feels abandoned by everyone, including his parents, sibling, teacher, and peers.

When Tyler's therapist asked him to draw a picture of his family, he drew a picture of himself, his brother, and his mother inside their home. He then drew a picture of the therapist at his front door, who was "stopping by to say hello." Tyler explained his drawing in this way: while the therapist was driving over to visit Tyler, a thumbtack got into a tire on her car and made it go flat. Her car is an old kind, made out of really strong metal. There was a star at the top of the car's radio antenna. Tyler went inside the garage, got brand-new tires for her, and changed all the tires. The therapist then left on a road safe to drive on. Below her was another road filled with cracks; she couldn't drive there, because it was unsafe. Tyler then colored in the cracks so that they were filled and safe. He announced that the therapist bought a monster truck and that it was now okay to drive on the road. Behind her was a small car that she couldn't see.

Tyler is stuck in a downward spiral. His underlying sense of shame causes him to act out, which then causes him more shame as he is shunned and ostracized by his classmates and family. He has lost his father to divorce and his mother to distraction. In reality, he has formed an attachment to his therapist, but in his fantasy the attachment is based on her need for him: he is powerful and can fix her car and the road.

Interestingly, the star on the antenna may represent the power or special qualities that in his fantasy he believes his therapist possesses. To be attached to a special person makes Tyler special, and to be the special person's rescuer makes Tyler even stronger and more special. Perhaps the small car behind the therapist that she cannot see is the vulnerable and weak Tyler he tries to keep hidden from both the therapist and himself. At the same time, the fact that he drew this little car for the therapist suggests that he also wants her to recognize how frightened, insecure, and alone he feels. He especially may want his therapist to understand that he is frightened when he lashes out at her for no apparent reason, as he does to most of the other adults and children in his life.

The Little White Knight Grows Up

A child's response to painful circumstances is not necessarily predictable. There are individuals who have positively adapted to the adversity they experienced in childhood, and others for whom similar adversity led to emotional hardship. We cannot predict a child's reaction to adversity, because children differ widely in their levels of emotional resilience. Many adults achieve a positive outcome in spite of their difficult childhood circumstances.

Similarly, a child who is a rescuer does not always grow up to be a white knight. People can benefit considerably from experiences and relationships during the course of their lives that can alter their unhealthy beliefs or behavior patterns. However, embedded in the hearts of all individuals are remnants of childhood experiences and the resulting vulnerabilities that require protection. The heart of the white knight and the self-protection that he or she characteristically uses will be considered in the next two chapters.

Summing Up

Childhood vulnerability as a result of loss, trauma or parental misattunement and a myriad of other factors may have led you to develop particular *character traits*, which are habitual ways of relating to others and to life in general. In the next chapter, we will more thoroughly consider how the traits of altruism and empathy affect white knight behavior.

Thinking About It

- What kind of models did your caretakers provide? How did these models influence the expectations and beliefs you have in your adult relationships?

- When you look back on your childhood, were you more likely to internalize your feelings or to externalize them?

- Think about the relationships you had with your peers when you were a child. Were you ever inclined to worry about your peers or take care of their needs?

- How attentive were your parents to your feelings?

- Did you misbehave as a child, and if you did not, what kept you from misbehaving?

- When you misbehaved as a child, what kind of response did your parents have?

- How often did you see your caregivers go out of their way to help someone else or each other?

3

Heart of the Knight

A white knight is driven to rescue. Whether she is rescuing her partner from painful childhood memories or spending hours designing her partner's website, rescuing behavior seems to be a basic part of her heart. This rescuing behavior gives the white knight a sense of pride and worth. Indeed, many white knights refer to themselves as an "altruist" or some equivalent, such as "a good man" or "bighearted." But what really motivates their rescuing behavior? This chapter looks more deeply into the heart of the white knight. We provide a background for understanding the white knight subtypes, and we examine how altruism and empathy relate to rescuing behavior in relationships.

Conceptualizing Altruism

Ellen, a thirty-four-year-old woman came in for her therapy appointment one day "completely disgusted" with her boyfriend, Chad. Active in various charitable organizations, Chad's generosity had extended to Ellen, and she often spoke about how indebted she felt toward him for all his support during her divorce and custody battle. The reason for her disgust became clear when she described watching a television program with Chad the previous night. It was an interview with a local philanthropist, and Chad had remarked, "That is just what I want to happen to me."

When Ellen asked him to explain, he said: "You know, to be on TV and have people honor me and think of me as an altruist who does all this good for so many people." Ellen was appalled. "How can he call himself an altruist?" she asked her therapist. "He's not doing his good deeds for the benefit of other people. He's doing his good deeds for his own good press!"

Ellen had inadvertently stumbled on an issue that theorists, philosophers, and researchers have debated for years: the lack of a consistent conceptualization of the term "altruism." The word "altruism" ultimately derives from the Latin root *alter*, meaning "other," and is defined as an "unselfish concern for the welfare of others" (*Webster's New Twentieth Century Dictionary, Unabridged*, 2nd ed., s.v. "Altruism"). The debate typically revolves around the issue of whether or not altruistic behavior, such as rescuing, giving, or doing something for another in need is ever truly unselfish, or if it is always unconsciously *egoistic*; that is, self-serving.

Egoistic motivations can appear in many forms. In Chad's case, at least one motivation was to be widely recognized as a generous person. An egoistic motivation might be the wish to avoid the pain of watching someone else suffer, to feel good about oneself for doing something altruistic, to avoid the guilt resulting from not taking a rescuing action, to establish oneself as dominant, to resolve some childhood trauma, or to vicariously have one's own needs met.

Nearly a century ago, Anna Freud (1936) found that her patients' altruistic behavior contained a powerful but unconscious element of self-interest, and represented internal conflicts. She believed that individuals, at times, surrendered their own needs for the sake of fulfilling the needs of others. However, she noted that this surrender actually led to the individuals' own needs being vicariously fulfilled through their identification with the person they were helping.

In contrast, some contemporary researchers maintain that altruistic acts do not necessarily contain self-serving or egoistic motives. C. Daniel Batson (1991, 6) defines altruism as "a motivational state with the ultimate goal of increasing another's welfare," signaled or evoked by an empathic concern for the person in need. Batson conducted many experiments that he believes demonstrated that altruistic acts can exist with minimal to no egoistic motivations.

Other contemporary researchers have postulated that altruistic behaviors have at their core a self-serving motive. This self-serving or egoistic motivation does not negate a person's conscious intent to help another. But it serves to clarify why some individuals in some situations may be inclined to rescue. Robert Cialdini and colleagues (1997) explored the sense of oneness the potential altruist can feel toward a person in need. A *sense of oneness* occurs when someone intensely identifies with another person. This intense identification creates within the observer a sense of merged or shared identities with the person in need. As a result, the observer's helping behavior—although outwardly aimed at helping the person in need—is inwardly designed to relieve her own stress created by her identification with the needy person.

Thus, if the distinction between the observer and the person in need becomes blurred, then the distinction between who is being helped and who is doing the helping may become blurred. If the observer's motive is to relieve his own stress, a stress resulting from the blurred boundaries between himself and the person in need, or in Cialdini's terminology, a sense of oneness, then the researchers conclude that the rescuing behavior should be considered nonaltruistic.

In Cialdini's experiments, people were given different imaginary scenarios in which another person was in need. Sometimes the scenarios involved a person in need who was close to the participant, sometimes it was a total stranger, and sometimes it was a casual acquaintance or friend. In general, the greater the commonality the participants felt between themselves and the person in need, the greater the likelihood that the participants would help.

Beth Seelig and Lisa Rosof (2001) conceptualized five categories of altruistic behavior. In all of the categories the conscious intent is to help another. The five categories range from the very common, instinctual, and normal end of the spectrum, such as a parent caring for and protecting an infant, to the pathological end of the spectrum, such as a psychotic person acting as the result of a delusion.

In the unhealthy categories of altruism, the individual projects her own desires and needs onto another person, thus symbolically making the other person into a narcissistic extension of herself. This extension gives the unhealthy altruist the ability to gratify her own needs through helping another, while consciously believing that her goal is to help another. In contrast, the normal altruist is able to distinguish the difference between her own desires and those of the person in need, and takes pleasure in helping the person in need to feel better and to achieve success.

Motivations are an important part of understanding a person's behavior. Although the white knight may consider his actions altruistic, we believe that his motives for rescuing are often self-serving. Realistically appraising what motivates your actions will give you information about yourself and help you learn how to stop your unhealthy rescuing. But what else plays a significant role in evoking altruism? Many theorists believe that the answer is empathy.

The Altruism-Empathy Connection

Rhonda, an overly empathic white knight, came in for her sixth therapy session very discouraged. During the previous sessions, she and the therapist had discussed Rhonda's early history of being abandoned by her mother and how this could be contributing to Rhonda's consistently poor choices in romantic partners. But Rhonda wasn't buying her therapist's interpretations. She believed it "just always seems to happen," and she described the events of the previous weekend to prove her point.

Over the weekend, she had gone to a party where several attractive and "together" men were present. Yet she had given her phone number only to Lewis, the one "loser" at the party, and he'd already "pestered" her into going out on a date with him. "Why does this keep happening?" Rhonda cried.

Rhonda and the therapist looked more carefully at what had happened at the party, and the answer became clear. While Rhonda was talking to a very attractive man, she had noticed Lewis awkwardly trying to engage in conversations with a few women, some of whom were already engrossed in lively conversations with other men. Rhonda had watched as these women quickly "blew him off," and Lewis, dejected but still hopeful, moved on. Eventually, Lewis made his way to Rhonda and the attractive man with whom she was conversing. Soon, the attractive man left the party, and Rhonda spent the rest of the evening at the party with Lewis.

What had happened? At first, Rhonda speculated that perhaps the attractive man had grown tired of talking to her and had used Lewis's entrance as an opportunity to make a graceful exit, but that still did not account for how Rhonda had ended up with Lewis. The therapist speculated that because Rhonda had not actively discouraged Lewis, the attractive man might have incorrectly assumed that she was interested in Lewis. "I wasn't interested in Lewis, but what was I supposed to do?" Rhonda asked. "I couldn't just blow him off. I just had this feeling."

We believe the feeling Rhonda had experienced was empathy. Lewis's socially awkward demeanor and his being rebuffed had triggered Rhonda's memories of being abandoned by her caregivers and had led her to identify with him, thus exaggerating her empathic connection. This empathy had propelled Rhonda to sabotage her goal of finding a suitable partner by the seemingly altruistic act of rescuing Lewis from an evening of humiliation. Ultimately, however, Rhonda's rescuing behavior was self-defeating.

Many theorists, most notably C. Daniel Batson (1991), have emphasized the role of empathy in altruistic behavior. Basically, Batson's empathy-altruism hypothesis states that your inclination to help another person is generated by your empathy for that person. Daniel Goleman, discussing the relationship between empathy and altruism, points to a process that relies on "three distinct senses: knowing another person's feelings; feeling what that person feels; and responding compassionately to another's distress...I notice you, I feel with you, and so I act to help you" (2006, 58). Yet Beth Seelig and Lisa Rosof (2001) assert that although empathy is a necessary component for altruism, in order to be a healthy altruist, one must be able to accurately assess the needs of another, as well as ascertain when and if to help.

We've already reviewed some of the issues in understanding the concept of altruism. Now, let's take a moment to look at empathy before we discuss the implications of the empathy-altruism hypothesis for our white knights.

Conceptualizing Empathy

Although the concept of empathy is generally defined as experiencing the feelings of someone else, various theorists and researchers emphasize different aspects. According to Heinz Kohut (1984), empathy is the basis of all human interaction. He referred to empathy as "the capacity to think and feel oneself into the inner life of another person" (p. 82). C. Daniel Batson (1991) defines empathy as experiencing the emotion of another person when the observer takes the perspective of the needy person. The strength of the empathic emotion depends on the relationship the observer has with the needy person, and the observer's assessment of actual need.

Martin Hoffman defines empathy as "an affective response more appropriate to another's situation than one's own" (2000, 4), and thus views empathy as a precursor to altruism. Nancy Eisenberg and colleagues (1989) consider empathy a vicarious affective response based on the awareness of another's emotional state. Across all definitions is the notion that you can feel, at a very basic level, the emotional state of someone you're observing, whether that someone is right next to you or on a movie screen.

Although you may empathize with someone and understand how he feels, you may not necessarily respond sympathetically or compassionately. For some people, feeling another person's emotional pain is so stressful that they will avoid that person. Other people may become angry with a person in pain, especially if that pain reminds them of their own. Descriptions of empathy have even included the notion that empathy can be used for destructive purposes (Decety and Moriguchi 2007; Kohut 1984). In some instances, people may exploit their understanding of another's emotional state to manipulate that person. The concept that a person can have the capacity for empathy, yet not be helpful in his or her response, is important for understanding the ways in which white knights protect themselves, which are discussed in chapter 4.

Empathy and the Brain

Most definitions of empathy include the concept of awareness or perspective taking, that is, seeing things from the other person's position. Thus, empathy has both a cognitive process (the ability to understand another person's view in terms of what the other is thinking or feeling) and an experiential process (experiencing an emotional response similar to the other person). For example, Patricia Oswald (1996) found that asking adult observers to focus on the feelings of the person in need made the observers feel more empathic toward that person, which in turn made the observer more likely to help. Asking the observer to focus on the needy person's thoughts also increased empathy and helping, but not as much as the instructions to focus on the person's feelings. Nonetheless, both groups had greater empathy and offered more help than the control group, which had not been instructed to take the other person's perspective in any way.

Because of this cognitive component to altruism, some researchers have investigated the role of the brain in empathic responding. When the empathic ability of patients with different types of brain injuries was compared, the researchers discovered that the location of the brain pathology determined which aspects of empathic responding would be affected (Shamay-Tsoory et al. 2003). Paul Eslinger (1998) studied a wide range of various brain injuries and their effect on empathic responding. He believes his results and those of other researchers raise the possibility that the cognitive functioning necessary for empathy, such as the ability to role-play or take another person's perspective, occurs in a different location of the brain than the emotional aspects of empathy, such as a sensitivity to what another person is feeling or experiencing.

We are hardwired to connect with another person through a process conducted by mirror neurons (Goleman 2006). A *neuron* is a type of brain cell that transmits messages. Researchers have discovered that if you observe another person performing a simple task, similar neurons in your brain will activate or mirror those of the person you are observing. This mirroring automatically enables you to predict the action and intention of the person you are observing (Gallese et al. 1996; Rizzolatti et al. 1996). Essentially, our brains "simulate" the feelings of those around us. This ability to simulate another's feelings enables you to reconstruct in your brain what another person may be feeling (Lundqvist and Dimberg 1995). Given the many and complicated interactions we have with other people throughout our lives, the ability to automatically understand what is basically going on with someone else is a crucial skill for successful social functioning.

Although you may be unaware that your brain is simulating another person's feelings, it can affect the way you feel. For example, when someone smiles, a certain pattern of neurons in her brain is activated. If you see that person smile, then a similar pattern of neuronal activation occurs within your brain. Emotions can be contagious, and neuronal mirroring may be, at least partially, the reason why we seem to "catch" a companion's emotions (Goleman 2006). Imagine a friend who is generally upbeat and generous, and always finds new and fun things to do. Spending time with him usually makes you feel energized, as if you have caught his positive attitude. You may have another friend who is generally depressed, negative, and pessimistic, and as much as you may want to help her, over time it's depressing to be around her.

By using this concept of neural mirroring, we can add a new layer of understanding to what Rhonda was experiencing when she observed Lewis being rebuffed at the party. In this conceptualization, mirror neurons in Rhonda's brain were activated in a manner similar to those that were activated in Lewis's brain, thus causing Rhonda to feel Lewis's discomfort. This mirroring of brain activation, plus her own history of loss, caused her to feel overly empathic toward Lewis and to behave in a compassionate, albeit self-defeating, way.

Empathy and the White Knight

As we've discussed, empathy is a complex process that involves biological, experiential, and relational factors. Let's look at the different ways in which empathy developed and is present in the white knights we discussed in chapter 1.

■ Sara: An Overly Empathic White Knight

From a very early age, Sara had witnessed her parents' financial and emotional struggles, and felt responsible for their happiness. As a result, she was inclined to become overly empathic and sensitive to what her parents needed. Taking over the care of her two younger brothers and the household would have been a daunting task for an adult, let alone someone who was still a child herself. But Sara's heightened sense of empathy enabled her to be a loving and responsible caregiver and to rescue her siblings in the way in which she would have liked to have been rescued. Sara became overly empathic, a trait that made it difficult for her, as an adult, to put herself first or find suitable, healthy partners.

■ Tom: A Tarnished White Knight

Tom's parents' self-centered need for their children to be academically superior had rendered them ill equipped to handle Tom's learning disability. As a result, Tom's childhood left him feeling shamed and inadequate. Luckily, his athletic skills were superior, and they became a source of pride. When he saw Nicole struggling with her knee injury, he was able to be empathic because Nicole's pain was physical, an area in which he felt especially competent. He used his empathy to gain her admiration and secure the relationship. But Tom also made Nicole so much a part of himself that when her needs differed from his own, he felt abandoned. Using his empathy manipulatively, he knew how to incite Nicole's insecurity with his criticisms and his involvement with other women.

■ Lexie: A Terrorizing/Terrified White Knight

Lexie had survived a terrible childhood plagued by abuse and neglect. Her caregivers had been unable to handle the basic tasks of parenting, let alone proper, empathy-promoting responses. Although her mother's cousin had done her best to provide Lexie with good parenting, by the time the child came under her care, Lexie had already been emotionally scarred. Consequently, Lexie, as a child, had been a bully and was very aggressive as an adult. But was Lexie really without the capacity for empathy?

Lexie began therapy with no remorse for her antisocial behavior as a child or an adult; instead she defended her actions with pride, explicitly stating that her loud, vicious insults and physically abusive behavior toward Jason had been justified. In fact, she said that if she had not behaved aggressively, she would have been a coward who had no self-respect. At the same time, she considered herself to be a good person, and cited many instances when she had clearly gone out of her way, sometimes at risk to herself, to help Jason or others. Even when she first saw Jason by the side of the road, she knew just what he was feeling and had decided to help because she knew she could.

It does make sense that Lexie, seeing Jason stranded, would feel some kind of commonality with him based on her childhood experience of being abandoned and afraid. It could then be argued that this commonality would give rise to a feeling of oneness, so that helping Jason was symbolically, and perhaps unconsciously, Lexie helping herself.

By looking at Lexie's history, we can see that in spite of her difficult childhood, when she wasn't feeling threatened, she would have an empathic response to someone in need and go out of her way to be of help. The problem was that Lexie often felt threatened. Nonetheless, when Lexie helped Jason, her conscious concern was for his welfare. Although Lexie was capable of empathy, how she used that empathy depended on the circumstances and how emotionally safe she felt. If she felt that Jason's suffering did not represent a negative reflection upon herself, such as his car being broken, she would respond in an altruistic manner. However, if Jason's suffering reflected badly on her, as in his withdrawal from her to pornography, she responded angrily and with the goal of humiliating and shaming him. So, Lexie had the capacity for empathy in spite of having had a horrible childhood, but her response to that empathy was complicated by her fear of abandonment and vulnerability.

■ Greg: A Balanced Rescuer

One of the components of childhood relationships that we discussed in chapter 2 was the impact of parents' discipline styles on the development of empathy. If a child had a parent or caregiver who encouraged her to think about the effect of her behavior on others, that child generally was more likely to be more empathic and to help others. Greg, the balanced rescuer, provides a good example.

You'll recall that as a child, Greg had been too afraid to visit his sick mother. However, when his father had talked to him about how hurt and disappointed his mother would feel if he didn't visit, he was helping Greg to take his mother's perspective and see beyond his own needs. Greg had then been motivated to put aside his fears, muster his courage, and visit his mother. He was then able to feel strong, brave, and proud of himself for helping her.

Greg had experienced significant challenges in childhood. His mother's illness had required her to be away from her family for an extended period of time, and later, his father had descended into alcoholism and depression. Nonetheless, both parents had provided a stable home with an emphasis on being thoughtful and considerate of other people and their feelings. Now, as an adult, Greg was able to be a supportive and empathic husband to his wife, as she went through her difficult medical treatment. He was also able to recognize his daughters' needs as they struggled to manage their lives and fears during their mother's treatment.

White Knight Altruism

The complexities of human behavior and motivation confound a pure definition of altruism. It can be argued that deep within a person's psychology, seemingly pure altruistic acts are actually driven by that individual's need, even if that need is to answer a higher calling. However, to insist on such a purity of motivation would mean that few, if any, acts could ever be called "altruistic." Nonetheless, at a superficial level, our white knights' actions and behaviors are altruistic; they chronically go out of their way, often to their own detriment, to enhance their partners' well-being. This concern for a partner's welfare, in part, fits some of the definitions of altruistic acts. However, it does not address the underlying motivations.

We will identify the white knight's rescuing behavior as altruistic if his conscious intent is to enhance the life or relieve the suffering of his partner. However, within the white knight's intimate relationships, we find altruistic acts driven by varying degrees of egoistic and unconscious motives that tend to be specific to the subtypes. These altruistic acts and unconscious motivations represent a continuum of egoistic needs; they are not discreet entities, and considerable overlap can exist.

Altruism and the Overly Empathic White Knight

The predominant unconscious motive for the altruistic behavior of the overly empathic white knight stems from her childhood anxiety about her caregiver's well-being, and her need to keep her caregivers strong and close. This behavior also represents an attempt at vicariously being rescued by rescuing her partner. She needs to feel needed and valued, but her main psychological conflict, the fear of loss and separation, motivates altruistic behavior that maintains a close connection to her partner.

This white knight's need to be needed causes her to be hyperattentive to her partner's needs. You'll recall that as a child, Sara was given the responsibility of caring for her younger siblings, regardless of how that responsibility interfered with Sara's own childhood. As an adult, Sara reenacted this model by finding partners who needed her help, which gave her a false sense of security within the relationship.

Altruism and the Tarnished White Knight

The predominant unconscious motivation for the tarnished white knight's altruistic behavior stems from the sense of shame and vulnerability he developed in childhood. Consequently, his rescuing is based on his need to maintain his partner's tie to him, hoping that his partner will idealize and validate him. For example, Tom hoped that by helping Nicole with her knee injury, she would admire and depend upon him.

Yet the intensity of the tarnished white knight's need makes him very sensitive to anything that hints of his own imperfection. Thus, an inadvertent slight by his partner can easily trigger his shame and cause him to become angry or hurt. If he feels the presumed slight to be especially severe, he may lash out at his partner or withdraw from the relationship.

Altruism and the Terrorizing/Terrified White Knight

The terrorizing/terrified white knight's unconscious motivation to rescue is an attempt to mask her intense sense of shame, vulnerability, and fear of abandonment. However, when the altruism of the terrorizing/terrified white knight fails to relieve her fear of abandonment because it has failed to obtain more dedication or greater subjugation from her partner, her response to that failure and disappointment is more extreme.

She may be compelled to control her partner in other ways, such as by threats of abandonment or by abuse. For example, when Lexie first became involved with Jason, she consciously wanted to be helpful. She described him as being "as cute as a puppy," implying that he needed her help, protection, and guidance. When Jason ultimately rejected Lexi's help, she became furious and was physically and emotionally abusive.

Altruism and the Balanced Rescuer

The altruistic acts of the balanced rescuer are predominantly motivated by a concern for the welfare of his partner. This concern may coexist with more self-serving motivations, but these egoistic acts are definitely secondary. Thus, when Greg, the balanced rescuer, would go out in the rain to get his wife a special cookie, he would teasingly say he was doing it for "husband points."

However, when pushed, he'd humbly admit that he did it because he knew it made his wife feel happy and special. More importantly, his major motivation to alter his work schedule during her cancer treatment was to increase his wife's comfort and to support her during a trying time.

The Complexity of Motivation

You've seen that our definition of white knight rescuing behavior does not require a certain type of motivation behind the behavior to qualify as altruistic. However, we do place importance on what unconsciously motivates the rescuing. Although we have emphasized particular motivations for each of the subtypes, the motives behind the white knight's behaviors are complex and multidetermined. Additionally, people are often not aware of what really motivates their own or their partners' behavior until time or other circumstances make it apparent.

At the beginning of Tom's involvement with Nicole, he had altruistically focused on making Nicole's life easier. Her knee injury had given her an obvious vulnerability, and it made him feel strong to help her. Unconsciously, Tom had hoped that his relationship with Nicole would erase his childhood feelings of being weak and inadequate, and in the process, make him feel powerful. Later, as she became busy writing her column and less able to attend his sporting events, he became angry and resentful, deprecating her work, and outwardly complaining about being unappreciated. Tom did not consciously set out to deceive Nicole or himself. The true motive for his altruism became apparent only over time.

Contrast Tom's altruistic behavior with Sara's. Sara had been raised to be a caregiver since childhood, and she felt guilty when she wasn't caregiving. This always led her to become involved with men who needed propping up, often to her own detriment. Sara needed to be needed, and she was amazingly successful at finding needy people. Thus, Sara's altruism derived from her anxiety about separation ("unless I am needed, I will lose the person I need").

The motivation behind Sara's behavior was predominantly based on fear of separation, while the motivation behind Tom's behavior was predominantly based on covering up his sense of shame. We deliberately use the word "predominantly," because in most cases, the motivations overlap. Tom truly did appreciate Nicole. Her ability to discuss sports insightfully, her spunk, drive, and creativity were all very attractive features to Tom. However, after Nicole gained success with her column, his hurtful behavior suggests that the predominant motive for his rescuing falls into the tarnished knight category.

Sara's need to be needed was apparent by looking at her history of involvement with men unable to successfully manage their lives. Such men were in need, which made Sara feel needed and hence safe. But Sara also felt shame from her early years as a result of her father's alcoholism and her family's circumstances. Additionally, she had been told directly and indirectly throughout her childhood that her needs were secondary, which gave Sara a sense of herself as unworthy. Although Sara's predominant motivation for her altruism was typical of an overly empathic white knight, there were also parts of her altruistic behavior that were shame-based and typical of a tarnished white knight.

Finally, consider Greg, the balanced rescuer returning home on a rainy night with the prized cookies, only to find his wife preoccupied on the phone and the children focused on a video game, leaving no one, save the family dog, to welcome him and exclaim over his bakery bounty. Even though he may have had the egoistic wish to acquire some "husband points," his predominant goal had been to make his wife feel special.

Yet in the face of his disappointment, Greg was healthy enough to let it go, because he knew that his wife's preoccupation wasn't about her feelings for him. He did not need to be reassured that he was valued with every interaction, freeing him to leave the bakery bag on the kitchen table and go watch a basketball game. Thus, in contrast to the terrorizing/terrified, the tarnished, and, to a lesser extent, the overly empathic white knights, the balanced rescuer can tolerate the disappointment of his egoistic motivations going unfulfilled, because egoistic motivations are not the predominant determinants of his altruistic actions.

Summing Up

The white knight typically sees herself as an altruist and an empathic person, especially in her relationship with her partner. This sense of altruism and empathy is a crucial part of her self-definition. What really defines an altruist has been the subject of much debate, as philosophers and social scientists grapple with the meaning of the various motivations that give rise to helping or altruistic behavior. We have therefore limited our definition of altruism to rescuing behavior where the white knight's conscious intent is to be helpful to her partner. However, the white knight's motivations and expectations reflect her core conflicts and often include the wish to feel powerful, needed, worthy, and safe. In the next chapter, we'll look at how a white knight protects and defends her sense of self.

Thinking About It

- How moved are you by the plight of another?

- Do you find yourself crying at movies when other people seem to be taking the character's predicaments in stride?

- Do you find yourself spontaneously helping your partner, even if your partner hasn't asked for help?

- In interactions with your partner, how often do you put yourself in your partner's place and try to figure out how he or she is feeling?

- When you help your partner, do you think about what benefit you will get from helping?

4

White Knight Self-Protection

Your rescuing behavior is influenced and shaped by habitual ways in which you protect yourself from emotional discomfort or pain. White knight self-protection is a response to real or imagined threats that may originate within yourself, such as a reaction to self-criticism, or outside of yourself, for example, in response to the possibility of rejection. Coincidentally, the ways in which you protect yourself can potentially interfere with the intimacy you want in your relationships because your self-protection may confuse, hurt, or offend others in the process. This chapter will provide you with a basic knowledge of what you are protecting, as well as an understanding of why and how you do so.

Your Self

During your young life you developed ways to protect yourself from emotional discomfort and pain. But exactly what is this "self" you are protecting? Your *sense of self* includes your perception of your attributes, talents, skills, ideals, and values; it is your *self-concept*. Essentially your sense of self is who you think and feel you are. Technically, it is a very complex mental phenomenon that develops early in life, and undergoes various revisions in adolescence and midlife, as well as in a life crisis. Psychological theorists have defined the self, for example, as the center of the individual's psychological universe (Kohut 1977), and as the composite of what you believe to be the characteristics of your identity (Morrison 1983).

When you were a child, you modeled yourself after the characteristics, features, and attitudes of your caregivers. These identifications with others created and modified your sense of self. Ultimately, they formed your *identity* as you took on those qualities as characteristics of your own unique personality and integrated them with your natural talents, abilities, and social opportunities (Erikson 1956). At times, you may be somewhat alarmed at the identifications you've acquired, or they may amuse you, such as when you think, "Oh my gosh! I sound just like my mother."

You may also find yourself *disidentifying* with a parent or significant figure in your life; that is, disowning an identification or avoiding identifying with that person by behaving in a contrary way. For example, if you had an uncharitable parent, as an adult you may go out of your way to be generous. Considering yourself as acceptable and being certain in your sense of who you are—having an identity and a set system of values—may determine your self-confidence and your ability to be in an intimate relationship without having a fear of humiliation, rejection, and, ultimately, shame (Morrison 1983).

Anxiety and Your Self

When your sense of self is threatened, you will experience anxiety. *Anxiety* is a state of fear, dread, or apprehension that warns you of potential danger, either real or imaginary. Anxiety will trigger various physiological and psychological responses. As a result, you may experience symptoms, such as irritability, anger, tension, difficulty concentrating, restless sleep, nervous energy, or agitation. Extreme levels of anxiety may result in feelings of emotional paralysis or emptiness. High levels of anxiety can also give rise to cognitive disorganization, depression, or disintegration (a feeling that you are falling apart or losing your sense of your self).

As a warning signal, anxiety alerts you to the possibility that something bad might happen, although you may not be able to discern exactly what it is that will occur. Because anxiety can feel so uncomfortable, you may try to make sense of it by attributing your emotional state to various things that are worrying you. Thus, a pain you feel in your chest might be attributed to a potential heart problem similar to what took place with a parent, rather than assuming its cause is indigestion. In relationships, you may experience anxiety as a fear of intimacy, separation, loss, abandonment, dependency, physical harm, or simply the fear of getting hurt if you fall in love. But you can also learn from your anxiety. A relationship that triggers your fear can provide you with an opportunity to think about and understand the origins of your anxiety, such as having been left or hurt by primary caregivers or feeling undeserving of love for various reasons.

The real or imagined dangers that evoke anxiety in overly empathic white knights usually involve emotional distance, loss or threat of loss of a partner, and self-criticism or criticism from others. Tarnished and terrorizing/terrified white knights have similar anxieties and fears, but these are experienced as more intensely threatening; that is, they carry the potential for shame or abandonment.

Responses to anxiety triggers vary. If you are anxious that your own flaws may be exposed, you may devalue others to turn the focus away from yourself. If you expect to be mistreated by others, you may be abrasive in your interactions with them. Or you may be controlling with your partner, because you are afraid that you will be abandoned if you are not vigilant. Although your response to anxiety may be emotionally defensive and can create conflict with your partner, it is really just your attempt to feel physically or emotionally comforted, in control, and safe. The self-protective maneuvers discussed later in this chapter are responses to anxiety, as well as to the guilt or shame that emerges when you do not live up to the standards of your conscience and your ideal self. Now, let's take a look at your conscience and see how it evaluates your behavior, and then at your ideal self, which stores and represents your aspirations.

Your Critical Self

Your conscience helps your sense of self decide if what you do is right or wrong and good or bad. Governing your thoughts and behavior, and evaluating your behavior in relation to others, your conscience is like a little critic within your head. When you fail your conscience, you feel anxious or guilty. Your conscience can be like the best and the worst of your parents. In fact, most of your conscience and your capacity to self-evaluate originate from your identifications with approving or disapproving parents or their representations in your mind. The rest is made up of other significant people and experiences that you identified with in your life, in addition to your basic disposition at birth.

Overly empathic white knights are driven by their conscience. They are motivated by anxiety and guilt, and feel terribly uncomfortable about any moral transgression or offense to another person. They try to be good so they will be acceptable to their conscience as well as to their partners. For example, one overly empathic white knight forgot to tell her partner about a phone message she had taken for him. She felt so bad about her error that she accepted his not speaking to her for the rest of the day as justified.

In contrast, tarnished and terrorizing/terrified white knights use various means to ignore their harsh, punitive conscience when their behavior, by conventional standards, is self-serving and does not take the needs of others into consideration. Disregarding his conscience, one tarnished white knight rationalized his sexual affairs by explaining that such behavior is acceptable in some cultures.

Guilt and anxiety can pressure you to seek forgiveness. Making amends, confessing, or apologizing for some action that your conscience perceives to have harmed another usually feels relieving. If you are prone to experience guilt, you probably have a tendency to accept responsibility or to accept too much responsibility when accused of wrongdoing. An overly empathic white knight is primed to accept blame and often feels guilty for actions that do not belong to him. You could say that he is overly responsible, doing whatever is necessary to restore his relationship with his partner, including inappropriately blaming himself, seeking forgiveness, and making frequent, if not unnecessary, apologies.

As we will discuss later, a tarnished or terrorizing/terrified white knight tends to feel shame, as opposed to guilt, in response to her transgressions, making her less motivated and less likely to seek forgiveness and to apologize.

Your Ideal Self

One significant way in which you define your self has to do with your ideals, ambitions, and what you value. Your *ideal self* is what you aspire to be, that is, the best that you think you could or should be. The ideal self tries to maintain or restore the feeling you once had, or imagine having, of being unconditionally loved and admired. At times, you may get glimpses of that feeling—perhaps if you receive an award that makes you feel as though you belong in the news, or at those times when you challenge yourself and succeed.

You have a capacity to evaluate what you think of your self relative to your ideal self. Your ideal self can be reasonable and attainable, or it can be inflated and unrealistic. However, objectivity about your self relative to your ideal self can be clouded or colored by your emotions and experiences.

The Yardstick of Self-Esteem

Your sense of self is constantly measuring itself against your ideal self and coming to various conclusions. If you measure up, you feel good, excited, even elated. If you don't measure up, you may feel depressed, angry, or ashamed. Self-esteem is determined to a great degree by your comparison of your sense of self with your ideal self.

Under ordinary, healthy circumstances the child gradually gives up his idealized view of himself and his caregivers in favor of a more realistic appraisal of himself and others. Thus, the values against which you measure yourself are likely to change as you mature and as you learn to evaluate potentials and accept limitations. If you have realistic ideals and can generally live up to them, your self-esteem will not be threatened. If your ideals are exaggerated and you cannot reach them, your good feelings from successes may be short lived, and you may feel that you are never good enough.

The continued hope for the impossible, the expectation that you will or can be unconditionally loved and adored, is not facing reality but rather holding onto an idealized image of yourself and an idealized version of what others can provide. If this is the case, your sense of self may be threatened by shame and its resulting depression, or by feelings of inadequacy for not living up to your unrealistic ideals. A better understanding of shame may help you recognize your tendency to hide what you feel from yourself and others.

Shame and Your Ideal Self

Shame is an issue for most white knights, just as it is for many other people. Self-critical judgments, or experiencing yourself as flawed or failing when you compare yourself to your ideal self, will lead you to feel shame (Morrison 1983; Wurmser 1981). In contrast with guilt, which has to do with behavior that violates your moral code, shame refers to your evaluation about some quality of yourself. When you feel guilty, you may want to punish yourself or you may fear punishment. Shame makes you want to hide yourself from others or simply disappear. Shame, in all of its manifestations, is a feeling you are likely to avoid, disguise, or ignore.

Andrew Morrison (1989) believes that shame is related to a feeling of depletion, a sense of emptiness that may lead you to feel that you lack value or purpose. Severe *shame sensitivity* results when parents or caregiving figures are misattuned and inadequately responsive to the needs and expectations of the child. As a result, the child learns that he is not worthy of attention, and develops an inclination to feel inferior or flawed. Thus the child makes sense of the caregiver's unresponsiveness or lack of relatedness by faulting himself, which both protects his inflated view of his caregivers and creates a lingering sense of shame within his self (Morrison 1989).

Life circumstances can catch you off guard in a way that can make you feel ashamed. Betrayal, loss in competitive situations, sexual failure, or the possibility that someone will discover your "secret" are examples of circumstances that give rise to shame (Zaslav 1998).

Shame can lead you to show no emotion so that you will not reveal any weakness, or you may be compelled to deny shameful feelings by acting shamelessly, such as behaving in an overly bold or pompous manner (Wurmser 1981). Tarnished and terrorizing/terrified white knights are particularly prone to emotions and behaviors that are reactions to shame. These shame reactions include anger, rage, contempt, envy, humiliation, emptiness, and depression (Morrison 1989).

Shame tends to get in the way of the ability to seek forgiveness, since a part of seeking forgiveness involves apologizing and admitting you were wrong. If you are shame-prone, admitting that you are wrong may be experienced as exposing your inadequacy, vulnerability, dependency, or weakness. Not surprisingly, the avoidance of sincere apologies in those who are prone to shame is often at the expense of their relationships with others (McWilliams and Lependorf 1990).

At times, it may be difficult to know if a feeling of shame is your own, or whether you have taken on a feeling of shame that belongs to someone else. In chapter 2 we described how a child sometimes experiences shame that actually belongs to a parent, which happens when children identify with parents who have addictions or whose behaviors are inappropriate. We mentioned in chapter 3 how one person can "catch" the emotion of another person. In this process, the person experiences the feelings of another, and may not be able to discern who actually owns that feeling. Consequently, a white knight who empathizes with her partner may experience the partner's feelings of shame as her own.

White knights have frequently told us about their feelings of shame that were based on devaluing themselves or assuming responsibility for the behavior of others. Some situations that have caused them to feel shame have included unfortunate family circumstances, molestation or abuse, having a parent with an alcohol or drug abuse problem, having a parent who thought of herself as unsuccessful, feeling inadequate because of learning challenges, or simply being the target of a sibling's envy.

Protecting Your Self

When anxiety, guilt, or shame is triggered, you will respond automatically in ways that will protect your sense of self. For example, when rescuing others, you can avoid your feelings of insecurity, weakness, and emptiness by behaving in a courageous or helpful manner, which then allows you to feel powerful, worthy, and fulfilled. Significant self-protective behaviors of white knights include idealizing, devaluing, avoidance, using controlling behavior, and withholding empathy. All of these behaviors involve the concurrent use of *denial:* a refusal or an inability to acknowledge reality when it contains unpleasant or unacceptable ideas, feelings, or experiences. Therefore, white knight self-protective behaviors include some level of reality distortion.

Idealizing

As a white knight, you are likely to have inflated or hard-to-reach ideals as well as a tendency to idealize others, situations, goals, or yourself. When you *idealize*, you represent something as far better than it is, or you portray a person as much closer to perfection than reality would indicate. The tendency to idealize colors the world, people, and even oneself in a falsely positive and impressive way. The inclination to idealize is present in most people, yet white knights tend to be particularly unrealistic in this way, and they often encounter disappointment because of their idealizing.

You may idealize others because of your own need to be idealized. That is, if you idealize someone else, who in turn approves of you or with whom you are associated, then you can imagine yourself as more important. You may identify with others whom you idealize, imagining yourself to have the adoration that you bestow on them. This is why children and adolescents want to emulate their music or movie idols: they believe that their lives might be perfect if they were adored in the same way that they adore their idols.

In many cases, identifying with an idealized person can be a positive force. For example, using another person as a model for what constitutes success or respect in your profession and striving to be like that person can motivate you to succeed. Yet idealization can also lead to envy and jealousy, as well as to disappointment in yourself. If you elevate another person to an ideal level that you feel you cannot attain, you may unnecessarily envy him and feel that you fall short.

Idealizing yourself can bolster your sense of feeling wanted, needed, and important, because idealizing masks feelings of weakness, envy, shame, and vulnerability. Idealization can be effective, because you will believe your own embellishment or version of the truth. For example, a tarnished white knight told us that women whom he viewed as especially attractive would always return his smile, because they "wanted" him. Another white knight reported pridefully that his girlfriend had called the previous evening to say, "I adore you, and I don't know if I can go another day without seeing you. Can we get together tonight?" On further inquiry, he clarified that his girlfriend had simply asked if he was free for dinner. "However," he noted, "I knew what she really meant," which was, of course, his idealized embellishment. His version of the dinner invitation glamorizes and romanticizes his relationship, portrays his girlfriend as needy, and allows him to idealize himself and be her hero by having dinner with her. Unable to simply enjoy the fact that his girlfriend wants to have dinner with him, he bolsters his sense of self by creating a scenario where she can't tolerate being without him.

Devaluing

Fearing any eruption of inadequacy, shame, or disappointment in yourself can motivate you to protect yourself by using *devaluation*. As the opposite of idealization, devaluation allows you to criticize or lessen the importance of someone or something, so that you protect yourself from feeling envy or jealousy. You are engaged in devaluing when you have belittling thoughts about another person, such as criticizing someone's attire, degrading a colleague who receives recognition, or diminishing a former partner of the person you love. Constantly evaluating everyone who crosses your path, devaluing a competitor, or diminishing the importance of anyone who might judge or evaluate you is simply a way to hide from yourself your own negative self-evaluation.

Provoking jealousy in a partner devalues the partner and can make you feel more powerful and secure. You may view your partner's jealous reactions as an indication of her love, and thus you feel reassured. For example, Ian, a tarnished white knight, was incessantly teased as a child by an older sibling whose approval he always sought. Hiding his own feelings of inadequacy, Ian teased and bullied his peers throughout his adolescence. As an adult, Ian found surreptitious ways to diminish and control others' self-esteem. He evoked in others the need for his approval, thus creating in them the insecurity he felt.

On one occasion, Ian complained to his therapist that the woman he was dating was excessively jealous and insecure. Ian's previous girlfriend had hurt and humiliated him by abruptly ending their relationship. Although his current girlfriend's jealousy annoyed him, it also made him feel secure. When his therapist asked about the circumstances in which his girlfriend expressed jealousy, Ian said, "Whenever I talk about my last girlfriend and how everyone thought she was brilliant, my girlfriend gets jealous and puts her down."

Ian was extremely jealous, envious, and admiration seeking. He evoked anger and jealousy in his current girlfriend with his provocative comments about his past girlfriend's "brilliance." Consumed by the fear that his own inadequacy would be exposed, and limited in self-awareness about the impact his behavior had on others, Ian was unable to appreciate how his statement had affected his girlfriend. Instead he felt contemptuous of her feelings, angrily stating that he was "just honestly reporting what everyone said."

This reaction to his girlfriend's upset feelings served to cover the shame he felt about her assertion that he was "insensitive and unempathic." Eventually, as her anger turned to tears, he felt sorry for her and guilty about feeling contempt for her. He then could rescue her by being comforting and reassuring. His shame about having been rejected by his former girlfriend, as well as having been accused of insensitivity by his current girlfriend, was then completely obscured by his white knight rescue of her self-esteem. Ian protected himself from his feelings of insecurity and weakness by minimizing his partner's self-esteem, thus causing her to feel bad about herself and needing him to rescue her.

Avoidance Through Addiction and Stimulation

Another white knight self-protective behavior involves participating in exciting, dangerous, high-risk, or self-destructive actions and distractions to conceal or avoid feelings such as anxiety, guilt, shame, or emptiness. Addictions, promiscuity, and even incessant socializing can provide an illusion of relief or create comfort by temporarily helping you avoid what you don't want to feel.

Substance abuse, as well as gambling, sex, or shopping addictions, mask unpleasant feelings often by creating a blissful state that is similar to the sensation of being surrounded by love as a child. In addition, addictions stimulate certain regions of the brain that can create inflated feelings about the self.

Intense sexual activities or affairs also can create the illusion that you are adored, and mask feelings of emptiness. If you lack a secure sense of self, you may rely on sexual relationships in an attempt to feel validated or stable. If you are unable to provide recognition or love to yourself, you may direct your energy toward gaining the approval of someone else. In a self-defeating way, you may seek stability through another person whom you have idealized (Teicholz 1998). For example, a woman who felt inadequate intellectually in relation to her husband began an intense affair with a man whose intellect she greatly admired and whose status she wanted for herself. Temporarily, she felt important and validated. However, relying on an idealized person for emotional stability is risky and unrealistic.

Anger

Anger can hide anxiety, guilt, or shame, and protect you from feeling fearful, responsible, or helpless, among several other possibilities. Since human behavior can be psychologically economical, there are times when anger serves more than one purpose. One white knight told us that when he forgot to do something that he had promised his girlfriend he would do, his instinctive reaction was to become angry with her and blame her for not reminding him, given his busy schedule. He later realized that he felt guilty for hurting her, shameful about being confronted, and fearful that she would distance herself from him, emotionally, sexually, or physically. His anger was an unhealthy and only temporarily successful attempt to protect himself from all three feelings.

White knights tend to use anger in various self-protective ways. Confronting or responding to a partner with anger, or maintaining angry thoughts about him, can hide from yourself the fact that you feel responsible for his feelings. Whether or not the anger is expressed, an overly empathic white knight may need to feel angry in order to justify leaving a relationship. A tarnished white knight may express anger when he feels shamed or humiliated. Fearing abandonment, the terrorizing/terrified white knight uses anger when he feels shamed or weak, and he needs to control the situation or his partner's self-esteem.

Volatile expressions of anger and hostility combined with a tendency to blame others often result from feeling shame (Zaslav 1998). If you are shame-prone, any accusation directed at you, regardless of how mildly it may be delivered, has the potential to make you feel that you have failed or that you are inadequate. Rather than simply admit wrongdoing, you get angry and accusatory in order to hold yourself blameless. Using anger or hostility for self-protection hides your vulnerability and needs. Unfortunately, since most people are repelled by an angry response, this method may be effective.

Your anger may drive away the very people who should know your real feelings, and it may deprive you of the opportunity to allow others to be aware of your needs. Behaving in an offensive or frightening way toward others can cause them to retreat out of fear. But, actually, the fear is your own, which you have turned against someone else in the form of anger.

Controlling Others

Both closeness and distance can be uncomfortable or threatening for white knights since either can evoke vulnerability. Intimacy may be threatening, because it creates the potential for loss. Emotional or physical distance from a partner may lead to insecurity that intimacy will not be restored. Controlling behaviors provide short-term security, because they influence both your own and your partner's feelings. You may use various means for control. For example, you may behave in an ingratiating way with your partner with the expectation that he will then want you; you may evoke your partner's sympathetic response so that she will remain close to you, perhaps out of guilt or obligation; you may behave in a way that incites fear, anger, or neediness in your partner so that he will need you; or you may provoke your partner to become distant from you when intimacy feels threatening.

If a current situation makes you fearful because it is reminiscent of an earlier trauma, controlling behavior can make you feel more secure. Controlling behavior in these situations may be your attempt to change the outcome from what happened in the past. In reality, the situation may not be within your control and you will again feel defeated.

An overly empathic white knight may altruistically rescue her partner, expecting that he will recognize her value. Her hope is that her helping behavior will secure their relationship. This behavior is neither intended to control her partner nor to denigrate his self-esteem, but eventually it seems to have that effect. By continuously rescuing her partner, she will appear to be the one who has all of the power in the relationship.

The tarnished white knight is skilled at controlling his partner's self-esteem. He has the ability to elevate himself in such a way that it diminishes her or requires her to want his approval. Keenly attuned to his partner's weaknesses, this white knight evokes jealousy and insecurity in his partner, which then enables him to be in charge of whether or not she approves of herself. Such control is malignant; thus, the partner of a tarnished white knight often struggles to maintain her self-esteem.

The terrorizing/terrified white knight cannot relinquish any power to her partner, because she fears abandonment. Perhaps the most unfortunate and unacceptable behavior that can result from this extreme need to control another person is the potential for physical abuse. A terrorizing/terrified white knight is not well equipped to deal with emotional distance from her partner. Vulnerability, shame, and fear of abandonment can lead her to become hypersensitive to disconnection. You may find a partner who will give up his autonomy and self-esteem in order to maintain a relationship with you. However, if you believe you are controlling his actions and feelings, you will never really know, or feel secure about, why he is with you.

Withholding Empathy

White knights can also use aspects of empathy for self-protection. As we discussed in chapter 3, it is possible to have empathy for another person without responding empathically; that is, you can understand what the other person is feeling without showing any sympathy or compassion. At times, your own agenda or needs may be so strong that you intentionally or unintentionally withhold your ability to empathize.

The concept that a person can have the capacity for empathy, yet not be empathically responsive, is important for understanding personality characteristics that most white knights have in common, namely narcissistic features. Before you decide that, of course, this does not pertain to you, allow us to explain. The label of *narcissistic*—a personality disorder characterized by, among other things, a grandiose sense of self-importance, an excessive need for admiration, envy, arrogance, and the lack of empathy that some have misattributed to it—has been used to describe people who seem oblivious when they hurt the feelings of others. Note that having a narcissistic feature as a part of your personality, that is, perhaps occasionally needing admiration or overestimating yourself, does not imply that you have a personality disorder.

It has become common to assume that a lack of empathic display is the hallmark of narcissism. But this is untrue. The criteria for the formal psychiatric diagnosis of narcissistic personality disorder in the *Diagnostic and Statistical Manual of Mental Disorders* for the American Psychiatric Association include "lacks empathy," but this has an important qualifier: "is unwilling to recognize or identify with the feelings and needs of others" (2000, 661). The unwillingness to empathize with another person is a feature of narcissism, but it is not the only criterion, and it is not the same as being unable to empathize with another person.

An overly empathic white knight may inhibit her empathic response when she ends a relationship. The guilt she feels about inflicting hurt on another person makes it necessary to protect herself from her usual readiness to empathize. In contrast, a tarnished or terrorizing/terrified white knight may withhold his empathy in order to control or manipulate a partner, or to justify his behavior.

Clearly, there are people who appear to lack empathy. Yet consider for a moment that perhaps these people don't really lack empathy, but instead, their vulnerability necessitates that they withhold it: they have an unwillingness to empathize rather than a lack of empathy. For example, if you and a person with narcissistic tendencies together view a news broadcast about a child abduction, she may express empathy or tearful compassion. This is possible because the situation does not directly affect or involve her, and so she is emotionally safe and capable of vulnerability. In the same way, many people who seem to lack empathy for the other humans in their lives can express enormous concern, sympathy, and compassion for animals.

The overly empathic white knight does not withhold empathy; in fact she would benefit from learning to do so. The tarnished white knight has an amazing ability to monitor his empathy, basing his willingness to empathize on whether or not it exposes his weakness or enhances his self-esteem. Yet when not threatened, his empathy can be evoked by a partner in need, because he has an inclination to be a rescuer and hero. The terrorizing/terrified white knight is consumed by his fear of abandonment, so he allows himself to empathize only when he can feel in complete control.

Trapped in the Armor: A White Knight's Dream

The white knights we have studied often refer to having two different selves. The self they proudly show to the outside world is the courageous, heroic rescuer. In contrast, the self they kept hidden inside feels needy and vulnerable. The following dream, reported by a white knight, illustrates that dichotomy:

> In the dream I am looking at a fallen knight in a suit of armor. I am trying to communicate with him. I am looking through the eye slits of the metal helmet. There is a little boy inside. He is tender, dear, and lovable and he can't get out. He is caught in there…that vulnerable little boy. He is trying to communicate with me and I am trying to communicate with him. I am trying to reassure him that everything is okay, because he is frightened.

Through his therapy, this white knight has come to understand and control his inclination to rescue, particularly his need to help women "feel adored." His need to rescue began in his relationship with his "depressed, temperamental, and histrionic" mother. At times, "she could be verbally abusive and physically rough." He felt very sorry for her, knowing that she had given up the possibility of a prestigious career when she married, had children, and moved to the country with her husband, who was kept away from home during the day because of his job in town.

Needing his mother's love, he became her "golden boy," providing her with the attention, admiration, and audience she seemed to need. At other times he would act out, making himself the target of her bad mood and verbal abuse, and then find ways "to get back in her good graces to make her happy." A version of this relationship with his mother persisted into his adult partnerships, as did his need to hide his helplessness and longing to be nurtured. Trapped in the armor of a hero was a vulnerable little boy who wanted to be rescued himself.

Summing Up

Your sense of self is at times subject to anxiety, guilt, and shame. Self-protective measures used by white knights include idealizing, devaluing, avoiding through addiction and stimulation, getting angry, controlling, and withholding empathy. We have illustrated how these self-protective measures are used. The next three chapters are extended case examples of white knight subtypes and will bring together all that you have learned about white knight behavior.

Thinking About It

- Who were the significant people you wanted to emulate in your life, and how did you identify with them?

- What characteristics of your caregivers did you avoid adopting as your own?

- In what ways does your conscience judge you harshly? Does that conscience have a voice, and if so, whose voice is it?

- Describe your sense of self and your ideal self. How would you characterize the disparity between them? What would it take to narrow the gap between the two?

- What self-protective measures do you find yourself using in your relationship? What are you protecting?

5

Knight Stories: The Overly Empathic White Knight

A heightened ability to empathize, a fear of emotional distance, and feelings of guilt are some of the main characteristics of the overly empathic white knight. She rescues her partner, hoping to be needed, wanted, and valued in return. Being overly empathic, she is especially sensitive to her partner's feelings and does what she can to be the source of his happiness.

The overly empathic white knight is the most common subtype of white knight seen in psychotherapy. His tendency to blame himself motivates him both to look within himself for the cause of his distress and to seek help. Often he comes to therapy feeling trapped in a relationship that isn't working out but feels too guilty to leave.

In this chapter you will meet Betsy and Ron, two overly empathic white knights who were unhappy and stuck in their relationships. Although their backgrounds and early life experiences were quite different, they continually chose partners who needed rescuing, hoping to create a relationship in which their partners would stay close to them.

■ Betsy

Betsy, a successful thirty-one-year-old marketing manager, came for therapy seeking help for the guilt and fear that prevented her from leaving Phil, her boyfriend of nearly three years. Hesitating to end an unhealthy relationship wasn't new to Betsy. Her track record with boyfriends was abysmal thanks to her consistently poor choices of partners. Betsy's history of failed relationships perplexed her, because she believed that she had always put her "heart and soul" into making her partner's life better, often at great cost to herself.

Betsy's History with Phil

Betsy had just come out of another disappointing and hurtful relationship, and was walking her dog when she met Phil, an unemployed computer game designer. At the time, Phil was living off the stock options he had acquired from his work at a start-up company. He had decided to leave the company so that he could develop his own computer game, which he felt confident would be very successful. Phil had been working with two collaborators on another game, but he'd broken off that working relationship because, as he told Betsy, they "just didn't appreciate the value of [his] creativity." Betsy, however, did appreciate Phil's creativity and she thought the outline for the game was "extremely creative and marketable." She also had been moved by his kind, gentle manner and his ability to "get" her. After a couple of casual meetings, Betsy had agreed to date him exclusively and see what developed.

What developed during the early period of their relationship was the sense that Phil truly valued her. After a hard day at her job, he'd listen to her woes, tell her she was wonderful, bring her wine and cheese, and give her a back rub. She was especially touched by his compassion when her dog was injured. Phil accompanied Betsy to the vet, visited the dog during the day, helped her clean the dog's wound, and gently carried the animal around until it was able to walk again. Betsy was so moved by Phil's caregiving that she ignored her concerns about his daily marijuana use and questionable work history. Instead, she focused on how she could help advertise and bring to market his computer game, using her skills and contacts.

After two months, Phil pressed to move permanently into Betsy's spacious condominium, noting that since he worked from home, he could provide her dog with afternoon walks and companionship. Hoping she had found a mutually supportive relationship, she'd agreed to Phil's moving in, and remodeled her guest bedroom into a work area for him.

Two years later, Betsy felt trapped and unhappy. The only progress Phil had made on the computer game he was designing occurred at Betsy's urging, and was limited to what was minimally necessary for the marketing and advertising plans she had created. Phil's lack of progress perplexed and frustrated Betsy. During the past two years she had tried various methods to motivate him. She'd hosted a focus group with all the teenage boys and young men she knew so that Phil could hear what they wanted in a computer game. She'd mapped out various timetables for completion of the different stages of the game's development and set up meetings with graphic artists. She had even purchased books on the history of computer games, and covered her walls with posters of the comic book superheroes Phil had told her were the inspiration for his game.

At first, Phil had seemed thrilled. He said he'd never known anyone so supportive, and in appreciation of Betsy's work on his behalf, he introduced a new heroine into his cast of characters named "Betts." Betsy remembered this period as one of the happiest times of her life. She'd thought she'd found a nurturing man who valued her, needed her, and was dedicated to the relationship.

Unfortunately, this happy period was short lived. As time went by, Phil seemed to resent Betsy's efforts, grunting out monosyllabic answers to her questions about his progress or saying he didn't want to talk about it at all. Betsy was especially hurt by Phil's minimizing the fact that his failure to deliver a prototype had placed her in an embarrassing position with the contacts she had cultivated for him, and had damaged her professional reputation.

Phil's failure to progress on the game was only one part of what was making Betsy miserable. His nightly marijuana use made her feel alone. His ability to understand her, which at first had made her feel loved and valued, now seemed to be used in a manipulative manner. On several occasions he brought up information she had shared about her family and history to negate her complaints about his marijuana usage, his lack of initiative, and his lack of participation in maintaining the condo.

It also seemed to Betsy that Phil looked for ways to diminish her. If she misspoke or mispronounced a word, he'd laugh and repeat it back to her several times. Betsy's friends, concerned about her well-being, asked pointed questions about how Phil spent his day, having seen him in the company of one of his ex-girlfriends. Several friends went so far as to say that he was "mooching" off Betsy and the lifestyle she was providing by allowing him to enjoy the comforts of her home, active social life, dog, and gym membership. Troubled by her friends' input, Betsy now wondered whether Phil's "gentleness" was, in part, a passivity that relied on other people, usually Betsy, to pick up the tab or take the responsible action.

Often, when Betsy questioned Phil about his activities, his face became red and contorted, and he yelled in an explosive temper outburst. For example, when Betsy confronted Phil about his contact with his ex-girlfriend or his lack of motivation to work on his game, he'd shout that she had no right to judge his life and would storm out of the house, leaving Betsy crying and panicked that he might not return. Several hours later he would return and tell her that she need not be upset any longer because he was back and the argument was over.

Recently, following one of these confrontations, Betsy noticed an e-mail on Phil's computer screen to one of his old girlfriends in which he made many unflattering and unkind remarks about Betsy. In the e-mail, he referred to Betsy's values as "superficial" and complained that she belittled him because he did not make enough money. When Phil returned, Betsy confronted him and asked him to leave. Furious that she had read his e-mail, he yelled that he had invested nearly three years with her and that she couldn't just unilaterally decide to end it. Sarcastically, he called her "Little Miss Perfect" and said she made "everyone" feel bad about themselves.

Perhaps what hurt Betsy most was Phil's accusation that all her marketing work on his behalf had put too much pressure on him and had made it impossible for him to proceed with his game. He then marched into his work area, where he spent the night. The following morning, he acted as though nothing had happened, and Betsy, overwhelmed by inexplicable guilt, was silent. One week later Betsy entered therapy, hoping to overcome whatever it was that was preventing her from ending the relationship and moving on.

Betsy's Previous Partners

Although Betsy had dated very little in high school, several of the boys she did date came from very troubled homes. One boy was essentially homeless. Betsy had located a social worker who found him housing. Her college boyfriends were often irresponsible, exploitative, untruthful, and, in retrospect, threatened by her success. The man she had been involved with before she met Phil was a successful orthodontist who had just emerged from a bitter divorce and was still traumatized by his wife's infidelity. Betsy had thought that once she helped him regain his confidence, he would be an equal partner financially, emotionally, and socially. She had spent many hours late at night on the phone with him, affirming how wrong his wife had been and how wonderful, smart, and interesting he was. After several months, his confidence apparently restored, he left her to pursue a relationship with his ex-wife's best friend.

Betsy's Childhood and Early Adulthood

Betsy's mother was a bitter and deeply negative woman who felt she had been cheated out of life's pleasures and rewards, most importantly, from her career as a movie star. The story Betsy's mother often told went as follows: She had been raised by relatives who treated her "like Cinderella" and had required her to take care of everyone else's needs while her own needs went unattended. After graduating from high school, she'd enrolled in acting classes and was working as a waitress when she was discovered by an influential talent agent. Through this agent she was cast in several commercials, and eventually, she'd landed a supporting role in a feature film starring a well-known actor.

One month prior to the shooting date, she'd discovered that she had become pregnant on her honeymoon. Although she'd begged Betsy's father to agree to an abortion, he had refused. Betsy's mother, fearing that she would lose her marriage if she had an abortion, walked away from her film debut and later gave birth to Betsy. When Betsy was two years old, her mother had planned to resume her acting career. These plans came to a halt when she'd pulled a back muscle, she believes while lifting Betsy. By the time her injury had healed, Betsy's mother had resigned herself to being a housewife, even though Betsy was an only child and her mother had no restrictions on her activities or any other major responsibilities.

Betsy's father, a baker, was a quiet man who had left all the parenting to his wife. Yet Betsy had fond memories of him bringing her special treats from his bakery, walking her to school, and sharing his dreams of developing a chain of bakeries. As time went on and her father's dream became a prosperous reality, he had spent less time at home, which had seemed only to increase his wife's bitterness and her need to blame others. Unfortunately, Betsy's mother seemed to focus most of her unhappiness on Betsy.

Even though Betsy did well in school, had friends, and was never involved in any serious rule breaking, her mother had frequently complained to her husband about Betsy's behavior. Betsy's father, who didn't really want to deal with his wife's unhappiness, accepted the notion that Betsy's behavior was the cause of his wife's misery, and then he became angry with Betsy. At other times, when he would leave for an extended business trip, he would ask Betsy to take care of her mother in his absence. What exactly this "taking care of" meant was never clear to Betsy since she believed her mother did not enjoy spending time with her.

In middle school Betsy had excelled academically and athletically, and she'd loved the accolades she received in the process. She also spent more time in after-school activities and hanging out with her friends. It was with her friends and teachers that her early rescuing behavior began. In her efforts to ingratiate herself into her friends' lives, Betsy had helped them with their homework and made them gifts. Wanting to be a model student for her teachers, she'd stayed after school to help set up for the next day or to clean up the classroom. She was also very aware of her teachers' emotional states and made an effort to anticipate whatever the teachers needed, be it coffee, help with organizing papers, or a get-well card.

One teacher who'd lived nearby became especially significant. Betsy had helped this teacher with difficult chores around her house, walked her dog, and pulled weeds in her garden with her. The teacher had tried to pay Betsy for her help, but Betsy had refused. Betsy enjoyed the contact, as well as the teacher's respect, advice, and friendship, which lasted for several years. This special friendship was very important to Betsy, but it made her mother jealous. One day Betsy overheard her mother complaining to her father that Betsy seemed more interested in helping her teacher than in helping at home, which Betsy admitted to herself was true. She had wanted to be helpful at home, but she couldn't tolerate the tension between herself and her mother.

Looking back at her early years, Betsy acknowledges that she contributed to the tension between herself and her mother, because she was angered by her mother's childlike and self-centered behavior. At times, Betsy tested her mother's emotional strength, hoping to discover that her mother really was stalwart. Instead she'd always found herself disappointed and somewhat frightened by how easy it was to provoke her mother. Dinnertime was especially tense, as her mother either tended to monopolize the conversation or sought attention from Betsy's father. Betsy recalled one evening when she had asked her father to explain how yeast caused bread to rise. While her father was focused on Betsy and her question, her mother had become visibly agitated, sighed, and blatantly tried to change the topic. Eventually, Betsy's father had stopped his explanation and refocused on his wife.

In spite of how difficult her mother was, Betsy felt guilty about her feelings toward her mother. In part, the guilt came from Betsy's awareness that her mother had tried to take care of her. Her mother had always made sure that Betsy was well fed and properly clothed, although Betsy recalled being teased because her mother was so oblivious to preteen fashion. Her mother had attended all of Betsy's sports events, even though Betsy remembered her mother criticizing and embarrassing her in front of her friends. Her mother had tried to converse with Betsy, but Betsy had felt so controlled by her that she'd withheld information as a way of maintaining some control over her own life.

Betsy's guilt was also compounded by her recognition that her mother was not like the other mothers she knew. Perhaps through Betsy's contacts with her teachers and friends, Betsy had seen and understood how socially awkward her mother was, how few friends her mother had, and how easily hurt and offended her mother could become at the smallest slight.

Some time around Betsy's thirteenth birthday, during the summer, her mother had abdominal surgery. Betsy's father was home for the surgery, but as soon as her mother was able to recuperate at home, he had left on one of his business trips. Betsy curtailed her activities and stayed home, cooking simple meals, bringing her mother requested items, and helping her mother to bathe and dress. Betsy recalled how confused and "creepy" she felt that her mother had so obviously enjoyed this care. Nonetheless, Betsy and her mother got along quite well that summer. Unfortunately, this period of relative peace was short lived. Once Betsy's mother had recovered and Betsy had returned to school and her own activities, her relationship with her mother went back to where it had been before the summer hiatus.

When Betsy entered high school, her relationship with her mother became very difficult. Betsy began to feel that she could do nothing right. Comparatively minor infractions—a bed left unmade, a towel left on the bathroom floor, chatting on the phone for too long—any of these would send Betsy's mother into an angry rage. Her father would return home after work only to find his wife in a fury that Betsy had inadvertently caused. Discounting how volatile his wife actually was, her father would then have a long talk with Betsy, angry that she had upset her mother. At other times, he'd come home happy, talk to

Betsy's mother, and then give Betsy the silent treatment, which Betsy found especially painful.

Betsy remembered consciously deciding that the only solution was to spend as little time as possible at home. She became involved in student government and various animal rescue projects, and worked for the school newspaper. The faculty adviser for the newspaper was a young woman who had recently graduated from college and was working at a local ad agency. As always, Betsy had befriended this woman and the woman, in return, became Betsy's mentor. Through her mentor, Betsy found a summer internship at an advertising agency, where she demonstrated a natural ability for making appealing whatever they were marketing.

Betsy did well in high school and was accepted at a well-respected out-of-state college. She remembered that her parents, especially her mother, had seemed proud of her acceptance and were very supportive. In fact, after Betsy left for college, her relationship with her mother had improved. They spoke regularly on the phone, but these calls often centered on her mother's complaints about her father. Her mother also became much more generous, sending Betsy expensive gifts and being genuinely interested in how Betsy's life was going.

During her college years, Betsy entered and won a number of student advertising contests. Her awards brought her to the attention of several advertising companies so that upon her graduation, she'd received multiple job offers. She'd joined an advertising firm, was given a very generous salary, and was soon managing important accounts.

Understanding Betsy

To the outside observer, Betsy had a normal and uneventful childhood. However, her mother's bitterness, anger, and resentful caregiving left Betsy emotionally neglected. Her father had been unavailable because of his preoccupation with work and his unwillingness to come to her aid. This had left Betsy with the unrequited longing for love, approval, and caregiving, so prevalent in overly empathic white knights, which had influenced her choice of partners.

Wanting to Be Wanted

From very early in her life, Betsy believed she wasn't wanted. This belief was a major contributor to her becoming a white knight. Betsy's sense of being unwanted primarily came from her mother's inability to be attuned and empathic, in addition to her unabashed acknowledgment that she had not wanted Betsy to be born. These maternal attitudes, combined with Betsy's father's absence and his collusion with his wife's behavior, only increased Betsy's belief that she was an unwanted child.

Even though Betsy's mother had been very self-centered, she was able to provide Betsy with the basics of caregiving. Nonetheless, her self-centeredness had interfered with her ability to provide Betsy with the sense that she was loved and valued, and held a secure place in her mother's life. Betsy had received some support from her father, but that had been limited by his inability to cope with his wife's unhappiness and his frequent absences from home. In fact, Betsy's mother, feeling cheated—and hence owed—had looked to her husband and daughter to nurture her.

Desperately wanting to be wanted, Betsy had searched outside of her home for caring relationships. Through her ingratiating and helping behavior, she'd made herself as indispensable as possible to her friends and teachers. During this process, Betsy had developed the belief that for her to feel secure in a relationship, she had to find situations where she was needed and valued for what she could provide.

When Betsy took care of her mother during her mother's recuperation, the caregiving roles were reversed and they got along well. When Betsy left for college, the tension between mother and daughter lessened. At that point, Betsy again became the caregiver, when she had listened to her mother complain about her father.

Betsy's Identifications

Betsy identified with her father's gentle and generous spirit, as well as his work ethic. Accordingly, she worked hard, consciously wanting to feel pride in her accomplishments. Unfortunately, Betsy's identification with her father also had some negative consequences, such as relating to her partners in ways that were similar to how her father had related to her mother. For example, just as her father had dismissed or denied his wife's less appealing qualities, Betsy denied and minimized her partners' problems. Similarly, Betsy was optimistic that her partners would achieve their dreams and be happy, in spite of all evidence to the contrary, just as her father had remained eternally hopeful that his wife would find some peace.

Betsy's positive relationships with her friends' mothers, her teachers, and the faculty advisor for the school newspaper had provided her with the sense that she was valued, and these positive relationships were also a source of identification. This was most apparent in her relationship with the teacher in the neighborhood, and later with the school's newspaper's young faculty advisor. Betsy had made this young woman a role model and even followed her career path.

Picking a Partner

Betsy was likely responding, albeit unconsciously, to the implicit memories that had been imprinted on her brain in childhood and to the apparent similarities between Phil and her parents. Phil was soft-spoken and seemingly gentle, and talked with Betsy longingly about his dreams. Betsy's father had been soft-spoken and gentle, and had talked to Betsy about his dreams when walking her to school.

Over time, Phil also showed similarities to Betsy's mother. He became humiliating, entitled, self-centered, and prone to angry, lightning-like temper outbursts, with no regard for the impact these outbursts had on others. Most remarkable was Phil's pervasive tendency to inflate his professional worth and blame others for his professional failures, just as Betsy's mother had done. Her mother remained convinced that had it not been for Betsy's birth, she would have been famous.

Another important element in Betsy's attraction to Phil was his inclination toward caregiving. Early in their relationship, Phil's caregiving became apparent in the attention he gave the dog and in the way he brought Betsy wine and cheese at the end of a hard workday, not unlike how her father had brought her treats from his bakery in her childhood. This nurturing had made it especially difficult for Betsy to leave the relationship.

Repeating History

As we go through life, we may become involved in relationships that appear to provide us with an opportunity for healing, but they have a fatal flaw that eventually causes a repetition of our early-childhood disappointments and traumas. Sadly, this was Betsy's experience with Phil. As her relationship with

Phil progressed, the unhealthy patterns that had plagued Betsy's previous intimate relationships appeared in her relationship with him.

Betsy had hoped that by fulfilling Phil's needs and helping him to reach his goals, he would love and value her forever. To this end, she idealized Phil and gave him emotional as well as tangible support to aid his success. Like a true overly empathic white knight, Betsy altruistically gave of herself, her time, and her emotions. Although giving in a relationship is part of being a loving partner, giving without reciprocity eventually erodes relationships and creates an imbalance of power that leads to resentment for both parties.

Ultimately, the pattern Betsy had intended to avoid by her rescuing behavior was repeated. In the past, Phil, like Betsy's mother, had blamed his failure to achieve on others, specifically his coworkers. Now he blamed Betsy. Phil could not acknowledge or appreciate Betsy's marketing talent, since it made him feel inadequate and incompetent. Rather than make the most of her ideas, he felt diminished by them, and then he felt compelled to diminish her.

Unable to Leave

If you had a good job, friends, and financial security, what would motivate you to stay in a relationship with someone whom you no longer respect and who diminishes you? The answer to this question for Betsy involves guilt, empathy, and fear.

Guilt and Empathy

Betsy grew up believing that had she never been born, her mother would have been famous and happy. Given the responsibility for her mother's distress, Betsy had been carrying around a strong sense of guilt for many years. Furthermore, as is often the case, this sense of guilt and responsibility for her mother's happiness grew to include responsibility for everyone's happiness.

Betsy discovered early in life that by rescuing someone else, putting another's needs ahead of her own, her guilt would temporarily subside. She had hoped that by rescuing Phil and making him a star, he would love her the way she had sought to be loved by her mother. Now Betsy was caught in a psychological vise. She had come to realize that Phil, like her previous boyfriends, really could not be rescued, regardless of how hard she tried. Yet her guilt prevented her from leaving the relationship. She felt guilty for "wanting too much," guilty that she wanted to stop rescuing Phil, and guilty that she wanted him out of her life.

Betsy's guilt was also tied to her empathy. An overly empathic white knight experiences and assumes responsibility for her partner's feelings. If Betsy left Phil, she would feel Phil's suffering, and then would feel guilty for causing it. Given the choice of living with her own unhappiness or creating unhappiness in Phil, she opted to stay in the relationship.

Fear

Betsy emerged from childhood unconsciously compelled to repeatedly prove her worth in order to be accepted and loved by a partner. This pathogenic belief led her to chronically rescue, and created a fear that unless she was indispensable to her partner, she would be rejected. Imagining that Phil was her "last chance," accentuated by his negative remarks about her, was another force that kept her in the relationship. Although Betsy realized that she would most likely find another partner, she couldn't escape her irrational worry that she would not be wanted by anyone.

■ Ron

Ron, a forty-four-year-old practicing psychologist, sought individual therapy to help him decide if he should stay in his thirteen-year marriage to his wife, Margot, or leave her to be with Valerie, a woman he had met at a professional conference. At the time of the consultation, Margot was unaware of Ron's involvement with Valerie.

Ron's History with Margot

Ron met Margot around the time he completed his dissertation. He had wandered into a local coffeehouse that was sponsoring a poetry event, when he overheard Margot reading one of her poems. Ron was so moved by her poem that he waited until the reading was over so he could introduce himself. Margot responded favorably to Ron's overture, and the couple began dating.

At the time of his therapy consultation, Ron still found Margot's poetry from that period of time, and especially her reading of that poetry, quite moving. Whenever he'd describe Margot's early poems, he'd put both hands over his heart and exhale a heartfelt sigh. Even though her poems usually dealt with difficult and painful topics— death, separation, abandonment, or fear—Ron found her "honesty a breath of fresh air" and was captivated by her "nuanced observations of everyday events."

When they first met, Margot was working as a library assistant. She had received an advance from a publishing house for her poetry book, but her writer's block and the resulting delay in completing her book had put her relationship with the publisher in jeopardy. As a result, she had become very depressed and was trying various antidepressants with limited success. Margot's mother had died when Margot was six, and she had struggled with severe depression on and off ever since her adolescence.

Ron believed that people used antidepressants too often when other interventions would work better, and thought that Margot had not had her psychological issues adequately addressed. He showed her relaxation techniques, talked to her about fear of success, listened for hours to her talk about anxiety, and quickly came to her aid whenever she felt that she was "slipping into the black hole." Whatever it was that Ron did and said, it seemed to work. Margot's writer's block lifted and she completed the book. Ron felt good, the publisher was happy, and Margot was so thrilled that she actually began referring to Ron as her "white knight," a title he readily and gallantly accepted.

Other than the out-of-town poetry readings that Margot attended to promote her book, the couple became inseparable. Ron had even rearranged his schedule whenever possible so that he could accompany Margot to her readings. Afterward, they would stay up late into the night discussing the poems and the impact Margot's readings had on the audience. Their sexual relationship was intense, and at the time, Ron thought Margot was "the most passionate woman" he had ever met. After a six-month courtship, they'd married. As a wedding gift, Margot wrote Ron a special poem about her love for and need of him, which he continues to carry in his wallet.

Ron dates the beginning of their marriage troubles to shortly after their son, Kyle, was born. The labor and delivery, which had been exceptionally difficult, had left Margot understandably depleted. Several weeks after the birth, Margot had become agitated, preoccupied with feeling worthless, and convinced she was unable to be a good mother. Ron had thought that Margot's difficult childhood was causing her distress, and he did his best to talk her through her emotional state. He'd also reduced his practice hours and hired a nanny for the time he needed to be away. Although Ron had been worried about Margot and the financial impact her condition was having on the family, he acknowledges that the situation gave him the opportunity to be the primary caregiver for Kyle, a role Ron had absolutely loved.

In spite of the hours Ron spent talking to and supporting Margot, and the fact that she had minimal child-care responsibilities, Margot's condition had deteriorated to the point where she became suicidal. Many of Margot's poems had focused on suicide, but there was something different in her talk about it now, which frightened him. At Ron's urging, Margot had consulted a psychiatrist, who'd recommended antidepressants. Ron's fear for his wife's safety overrode his dislike of antidepressants, and he'd reluctantly agreed to the treatment plan. Several weeks later, Margot's suicidal thoughts had abated, and she took over some of the child care.

Even with the antidepressants, Margot had still struggled. Dealing with Kyle, now an active and precocious two-year-old, had overwhelmed her. At least once a week, she'd placed an emergency call to Ron, demanding that he come home and help. Ron had felt that Kyle was just being a two-year-old, but he recognized that Margot could not handle the child. Margot's psychiatrist started seeing her for weekly psychotherapy sessions and changed her medication. In addition, to further relieve Margot's stress, Ron had found a day care facility that Kyle could attend while Ron was at work.

In many ways, matters calmed down, and Ron hoped that life would go back to what it had been prior to Kyle's birth. Now, during the limited time Margot spent alone with Kyle, she enjoyed their son and took delight in his discovery of his world. As Kyle got older and Margot gained confidence, they had developed a fun and caring relationship. Indeed, Kyle became the center of her life.

Margot's emergency phone calls had stopped, her late-night ruminations that had kept Ron up for hours were gone, she had made friends with other mothers through Kyle's lower school, and she worked on several school committees. Between playing with Kyle, and attending to her school committee responsibilities and her writing, Margot had no free time. Yet, she seemed happy. When Ron asked her about the "black hole" that had so troubled her in the past, she'd simply wave him off and change the topic. But, although life had seemed to settle down, Ron was unhappy. He felt lonely and excluded from Margot's real feelings, and he believed that an emptiness had descended upon their marriage.

The Achilles' heel to Margot's newfound peace was her poetry. She had returned to writing, but she now wrote about the joy of motherhood and what Kyle was teaching her about life. Unfortunately, this new subject matter was not what her publisher wanted, which made Margot prickly and irritable. Ron believed the reason the poetry wasn't going well was because it lacked any real feeling or "inner truth," and he described it to his therapist as having a "greeting card mentality."

Given Ron's assessment of her poetry, it is not surprising that his suggestions were met with hostility and accusations. Ron was especially hurt by Margot's response to his suggestion that she should return to her old concerns and write about existential issues as opposed to her current focus on parenthood. Margot responded harshly to this suggestion, accusing Ron of liking it better when she was depressed so that he could be "the big strong know-it-all shrink!"

Over the next year or so, Ron, feeling rejected, hurt, lonely, and misunderstood, retreated from the marriage, focusing instead upon his practice and his relationship with Kyle. Ron and Kyle spent many hours building birdhouses, going for walks, and feeding the ducks at a nearby pond. During this time, Ron's relationship with Margot deteriorated even further. Their sexual life was nonexistent, and Margot, sensing his deliberate physical and mental absence, escalated their disagreements, most likely trying to get Ron to pay attention to her but, in reality, only pushing him farther away.

As the couple entered their twelfth year of marriage, they tried couples therapy. The therapy seemed to reduce the number of angry outbursts, but by that point Ron had concluded that he had made a terrible mistake in marrying Margot. According to Ron, Margot was simply "wired" differently than he. He believed she lacked insight and empathy, which prohibited any productive use of couples therapy. He also said that he was tired of being the caregiver and that he wanted a relationship with an "equal."

Feeling hopeless and alone, Ron went to a professional seminar to learn more about a new psychotherapy technique that he could use in his practice. At one of the lectures, the instructor asked for volunteers to role-play an unhappy husband and a therapist. Ron volunteered to play the husband, and Valerie, a psychiatric nurse, volunteered to play the therapist. The instructor told Ron to use material from one of Ron's cases, but Ron soon found himself using his own life for the role.

Ron was amazed at how quickly Valerie, as the "therapist," understood what was going on with him. After the seminar, the two chatted, and he learned that Valerie's insights came from her own experience of feeling ignored and exploited by her partner. Her relationship had recently ended, and she was just coming out of a severe depression that had led her to resume her alcohol use. Nonetheless, he described Valerie as "warm, insightful, and sexy."

He was aware that Valerie had her own set of problems but quickly added that she was very strong and was well on her way to getting her life back on track. He did agree that her frequent phone messages after she had been drinking and her hesitation to return to Alcoholics Anonymous (A.A.) could become problems, but he minimized his concerns, adding, "Who doesn't have baggage?"

Ron's Previous Partners

When Ron chronicled his relationships prior to Margot, a pattern of choosing needy, depressed women emerged. His most significant relationship in high school had been with a classmate who was struggling with the aftereffects of having been sexually abused by her stepfather. In college and graduate school, his significant relationships were with a woman had been overtly suicidal, a woman who was significantly depressed, and a third woman who had required a hospitalization due to ingesting LSD, which Ron claimed she had not knowingly taken. In spite of these obvious difficulties, Ron described these women as fun, empathic, and, at least in the beginning, very sexy. However, the quality that he found most attractive in all three women was their "vulnerability." He believed that he had made a positive impact on their lives but that, over time, that influence had gone unappreciated.

Ron's Childhood and Early Adulthood

Ron grew up in a stable, middle-class home. His father had been an insurance claims adjuster, and his mother a social worker. Ron had gotten along well with his brother, who was four years younger. Neither his father nor his mother had ever abused drugs or alcohol, and they were never overtly depressed. However, his mother frequently told stories about her very difficult childhood, and these stories had made a significant impact upon him.

Ron's mother had been raised in a poor and crime-ridden part of town plagued by gangs and arson, and she had experienced the terrible trauma of witnessing her own mother being killed when they had entered a grocery store that was being robbed. In a tragic twist of fate, Ron's grandfather had died a year and a half later from lung cancer. Somehow, by working odd jobs and staying with friends, Ron's mother had completed high school and college, where she'd met Ron's father.

In spite of her childhood hardships, she and her husband had created a loving home. Ron's father was a very stable and dependable man who'd enjoyed hands-on remodeling, so there was always a room under construction in their home. Shy and reserved, Ron's father had appreciated his wife's spunk and the friends and social life she brought into his life. However, everyone in the family agreed that Ron's mother was someone who could just not sit still. She always had too many things on her plate, yet was always eager to help someone else. She was well liked and respected in the community, which had made Ron and his brother very proud. At other times, however, he had felt abandoned because of all her activities, and as he got older he'd worried about her inability to relax. In spite of Ron's concerns about his mother's rescuing, he attributes all that he has ever achieved to her and her positive can-do attitude.

What probably had the largest impact on Ron's white knight development was his mother's need to tell and retell stories from her difficult and frightening childhood. When she would start her storytelling, his father would quietly retreat to his remodeling work, usually followed by Ron's younger brother. Years later, Ron asked his father why he had always left and wouldn't stay to listen to the stories. "I saw that the listening didn't help her," his father had explained, "and it just hurt too much to hear them."

But Ron did stay and listen. He'd felt that his mother "needed to tell the story and have someone there to hear it." Ron listened while they did the dishes, ran errands, or in those rare moments when Ron's mother relaxed over a plate of cookies; and in the process Ron felt strong, helpful, and special.

Yet the stories also had a negative impact on him. He suffered from several phobias, was terrified when he heard a fire truck siren, and became so anxious when either parent had a cold that he would develop stomach pain, which often sent him home from school. When he was eleven, his concern about his parents' health caught the attention of a school counselor, who had referred him to a psychologist. Ron had met with the psychologist for over a year. The psychologist also had met with Ron's mother and, on several occasions, had met with Ron and his mother together.

During one of these joint meetings, Ron's mother's storytelling was discussed. Ron can't remember what was said in that meeting, but he does remember that afterward the storytelling stopped. Over the course of the therapy, his phobias had seemed to abate. He did well in middle and high school, had friends, and was on the varsity track team. He also wanted to be perfect, so his mother wouldn't have anything more to worry about. To this day he views his mother with both awe at how she overcame such hardships and concern that she must live with such terrible childhood scars.

Ron attended college, where he did well academically and socially. He felt so helped by the therapy he'd received as an adolescent that he declared psychology as his major and attended graduate school for his Ph.D.

Understanding Ron

You can easily see why we call Ron a white knight. He had demonstrated chronic rescuing behavior with his girlfriends and his wife; Margot even called Ron her "white knight." Although we know little about Valerie, what we do know suggests that she was struggling with depression and alcoholism, and as evidenced by her frequent messages to Ron, she was also seeking rescue. Ron had an excessive need to be needed. He identified with his mother's loss and thus feared loss and separation himself. He denied the reality of his partners' issues and was hyperattuned to their needs. And, finally, he repeatedly found partners who needed rescuing.

How did Ron end up as a white knight? Both of Ron's parents were very present in his life, without any extreme pathology that would have made them unavailable. They had treated him lovingly and with respect. However, his mother, unaware that she was overwhelming her family, had told and retold the stories of her own traumas, and in the process significantly contributed to Ron's overly empathic behavior.

The Family's Listener

Ron's father couldn't listen to his wife's stories; it had hurt him to hear his wife's pain. Instead, with his younger son at his side, Ron's father tore down walls and installed new plumbing. As the family's listener, Ron had been an overly empathic white knight in training. He listened not only because it was his role but also because of his empathy for his mother. Ron's empathy had led him to take action, and the action that he took was listening. He listened so that his mother could be heard and not be left alone with her memories. Unfortunately, his role as the listener was overwhelming and made him highly anxious.

Anxious to Be Close

Ron's mother's accounts of her childhood had been a major source of anxiety for Ron. These stories described a world where danger lurked behind every corner and parents were unable to protect their children because of circumstances beyond their control or awareness. In reality, it was a world far different from Ron's safe, middle-class, early home life. Nonetheless, the stories had unintentionally overstimulated Ron, and made him feel anxious and vulnerable. Ron had handled his anxiety and vulnerability about his mother's and his own well-being by staying close to her and being her support. Moreover, when Ron had helped and protected his mother, he'd increased her ability to help and protect him, which had reassured and comforted him.

Another source of Ron's anxiety was his identification with his mother. Ron had made his mother's childhood world his world. This identification was most obvious in his childhood fears. For example, he was frightened by fire trucks, much as his mother must have been frightened living in a neighborhood plagued with arson. He was overly concerned about his parents' health, most likely fearing that his mother and father would die and leave him, as his maternal grandparents had left his mother. Ron's rescuing of his mother, his young classmates, and later his girlfriends and wife can also be seen as an identification with his mother's chronic rescuing.

As a child, Ron had often felt that anyone in greater need than he would get his mother's attention. Although he may have resented his mother's absence when she was away rescuing, he had learned the lesson that good people rescued, and Ron aspired to be good. He also had understood that when his mother was altruistically rescuing others, she was unconsciously rescuing her childhood self.

Needing to Be Needed

When Ron went to college, he'd declared psychology as his major. He had been so helped by the therapy he had received as a child that he wanted to help others. But for Ron, it wasn't simply a profession. Continuing the pattern of what love was for him, Ron needed to be needed. What better profession to fulfill Ron's needs than to be someone who helps by listening?

Ron's need to be needed also influenced his choice of romantic partners. His attraction to needy women paralleled his relationship with his mother, where Ron was the altruistic rescuer and his mother was the needy person. Although Margot's childhood traumas differed from those of Ron's mother, both women had lost their mothers at an early age, which had left them frightened and vulnerable. Margot, like his mother, wore her emotions on her sleeve, literally, in both uses of the word, "broadcasting" her emotions to the world. Hearing Margot read her poetry must have been like reliving the storytelling with his mother. No wonder Ron had felt such a tug at his heart.

Ron was especially attracted to vulnerable women. Margot's vulnerability had given Ron the sense of being helpful and effective, but it also had provided him with the sense that he was powerful and in control. For Margot, Ron had provided the nurturing and care that she had been denied in childhood, and she'd adored him for it. It seemed a match made in heaven until Margot, through the use of antidepressants, psychotherapy, and perhaps her relationship with Kyle, no longer felt helpless and vulnerable.

Margot's improved mental health left Ron feeling that there was no role for him in her life if he wasn't rescuing her. For example, when Margot wanted to write about the joys of being a mother, Ron had felt lonely and no longer needed. This discomfort most likely prompted his suggestion that Margot should return to her earlier poetry subjects of bleak topics, since that would reinstate their previous relationship in which he had felt secure and in control.

Margot may have been quite right when she fired back that Ron liked it better when she was depressed so that he could be the strong one. Ron had felt rejected and feared that his connection with Margot was slipping away once she was no longer so needy. His subsequent withdrawal did evoke anxiety in Margot, but rather than make her feel more in need of him, it had made her angry and aggressive.

Staying in the Marriage

Several important issues kept Ron in his marriage, and they all contained an element of guilt, empathy, or fear. The first reason Ron stayed was his relationship with his son. He was very attached to Kyle, and the idea of being separated from him was intolerable. He also empathized with Kyle, and worried how a divorce and custody arrangement would affect Kyle and their relationship. Perhaps most importantly, Kyle was the center of Ron's life, and Ron would have done anything to keep the child happy and safe.

Ron empathized with Margot too, and he felt guilty about the pain he anticipated causing her if he left the marriage. Additionally, if we understand her to be a representation of Ron's mother, it would be very difficult for Ron to leave Margot. Given that Ron's self-esteem was partly based on being his mother's rescuer and protector, he could not tolerate the separation.

Considering himself to be an honorable person, Ron was also guilt ridden about his relationship with Valerie. Living a double life was at great disparity with his conscience and his ideals, and gave rise to much guilt and confusion.

Idealizing or Devaluing His Partners

To handle his guilt and justify his infidelity, Ron currently idealized Valerie and devalued Margot. Margot had always been open about her emotional troubles, and well into their marriage these emotional troubles had not dampened Ron's love for her. In fact, for many years, Ron had idealized Margot, viewing her vulnerability as tragically romantic, insightful, and indicative of a greater understanding of the world. When Margot had become unstable, Ron had easily assumed the role of caregiver for both his son and wife without complaint. Indeed, he had relished the role.

In the past several years, however, Margot had been managing quite well, and Ron's role as rescuer had been substantially diminished. But instead of enjoying Margot's increased self-confidence, Ron had felt shut out and concluded that he and Margot were incompatible, a conclusion that covered over his anxiety that she no longer needed him.

Ignoring the warning signs—Valerie's numerous phone messages, her alcoholism, and her reluctance to return to A.A.—Ron now idealized Valerie. He saw Valerie as strong and stable, which made him feel that he had found an equal. He believed that her insights revealed her "incredibly empathic nature," which made him feel understood. He viewed the intensity of their sexual relationship as an indication of her passion, which made him feel powerful and manly.

Ron's idealization of and lust for Valerie would inevitably lead to a repetition of the disappointment and defeat he had felt with Margot. Consciously, Ron was trying to find a different kind of partner. Unconsciously, he was repeating the pattern of rescue that began in his childhood when he had idealized his mother to protect himself from the disappointing and frightening truth—that his mother was too needy to rescue the vulnerable boy who posed as her confidant and hero.

Overly Empathic Patterns

Betsy and Ron came from very different types of homes, and yet they both found themselves chronically rescuing their partners. Let's look at some of the similarities and differences between these two people and try to understand how they both ended up in such unhealthy relationships.

Needing to Be Needed

Both Betsy and Ron had developed a need to be needed. Betsy's need came out of the belief that she had not been wanted, so she had to make herself desirable and worthy by recognizing and fulfilling other people's needs. Ron's need arose from having been tacitly assigned to the role of his mother's protector. However, behind both sets of these motivations was the need to be close to their caregivers or partners in order to have their own needs met. For Betsy, given her mother's rejecting resentment, it was a need to be close to her teachers, friends, and mentors. For Ron, it was a need to be close to his mother to keep her safe.

Picking a Partner

Both Betsy and Ron chose needy partners who had personality characteristics similar to their parents and who were only marginally managing their lives. Phil had elements of both of Betsy's parents. Margot had many similarities to Ron's mother. However, both Phil and Margot were people in need. Their similarities to Betsy's and Ron's defective childhood caregivers exaggerated the empathy Betsy and Ron felt toward their partners and heightened their tendency to rescue. By rescuing others and making themselves indispensable, both Betsy and Ron had hoped to create a secure and lasting connection with their partners and ensure that their partners would be strong enough to provide them with love and security in return.

Rescuing Behaviors and Results

Although both Betsy and Ron engaged in rescuing, how they rescued and the success of their rescue efforts were different. In spite of these differences, the overall impact of their rescuing behavior on their relationships was similar. Betsy rescued Phil by providing a comfortable life and trying to help him achieve his dream, thus compensating for her undeserved guilt over her mother's failure to achieve her dream. Ron rescued Margot by providing emotional comfort, support, and stability as he had done for his mother.

Betsy's rescue attempts made Phil feel judged, criticized, inadequate, and incompetent. But Betsy's rescue attempts also made her feel frustrated, betrayed, unfairly attacked, unappreciated, and diminished. Ron's rescue attempts, which included getting Margot appropriate psychiatric medication and counseling, may actually have contributed to Margot's increased self-esteem, stability, and competence.

Unlike Betsy's rescuing, in some ways, Ron's rescuing was actually success-ful. Nonetheless, Ron became unhappy, lonely, and provocative as Margot's depression lifted, probably because her improvement upset the balance in their marriage. We can only wonder what would have happened to their marriage if Margot had not improved: would Ron have been happy remaining the care-giver or would he have become resentful?

And what about Betsy? If Phil had become more proactive and taken on more responsibility for his own life, would Betsy have been happy? Would she have continued to be obsessively involved in the game, unable to let Phil have his success, or would she have withdrawn, worrying that she was no longer needed? Or would she have felt proud and secure? Clearly, there is no way for us to know for sure. What we do know is that in spite of all their giving and rescuing, both of these white knights ended up defeated.

Trapped by Empathy and Guilt

Although their lives took different paths, both Betsy and Ron found them-selves guilt-ridden and unable to leave their unhappy relationships. This is one of the more predictable results of the overly empathic white knight's rescuing efforts. Remember that the overly empathic white knight anticipates as well as empathizes with her partner's feelings. Although most of us try to consider the emotional impact our behavior will have on our partners, the extreme empathy of this white knight creates a hyperawareness of her partner's emotions. As unhappy as Betsy and Ron became in their relationships, living with their own unhappiness was preferable to living with the pain they anticipated they would cause their partners. As a result, they remained in their relationships, trapped by their own guilt and empathy.

Summing Up

The overly empathic white knight chooses a partner who has a need he believes he can fulfill. To that end, he strives to be good, helpful, and caregiving in an attempt to make himself indispensable and to ensure their connection. Predictably, his seemingly altruistic, overly empathic, overly responsible, and self-sacrificing behavior creates resentment and bitterness that leads to unhappiness for himself and his partner.

In the next chapter you will meet two tarnished white knights. In contrast to the overly empathic white knight, a major source of stress in relationships for the tarnished white knight is his fear that his weakness, vulnerability, or inadequacy will be exposed.

Thinking About It

- How self-sacrificing have you been in order to maintain your connection with your partner?

- How do your partner's feelings affect your feelings?

- If your partner is in a bad mood, how driven are you to try to make him or her feel better?

- Have you stayed in a relationship because you felt guilty about the pain you would cause your partner if you left him or her?

- Have you stayed in a relationship because you believed that it was your last chance to find a partner?

- How do you feel when you are the caregiver in a relationship?

6

Knight Stories: The Tarnished White Knight

The tarnished white knight seeks a partner who will validate and admire him, but often finds himself needing more attention than his partner is able to give. Typically, the tarnished white knight seeks therapy when he feels empty or depressed, when he wants to "fix" a partner whom he feels is unappreciative and unhappy, when his partner threatens to leave the relationship, or when his child needs help.

Regardless of her motivation for entering therapy, the tarnished white knight's struggle with her vulnerability and sense of inadequacy permeates her intimate relationships. In this chapter you will be introduced to Brad and Kimberly, two tarnished white knights. Brad had an unrealistic vision of who he was and who he should be, based on his parents' expectations and his mother's extreme adoration of him. In contrast, Kimberly felt inadequate and flawed due to her mother's history and behavior, along with her stepfather's criticisms and his need to view her as an extension of himself. Looking to relationships as a way to overcome their feelings of inadequacy, both Brad and Kimberly sought partners who needed rescuing and who would confirm their self-worth.

■ Brad

Forty-five-year-old Brad owned a nutritional supplement store. He and his wife, Patricia, had been married for fifteen years. They sought couples therapy because of Patricia's unhappiness and her suspicion that Brad was having an affair with his chiropractor, a suspicion that Brad had claimed was unfounded. Patricia believed Brad stayed in their marriage because of her modest but needed trust fund. Brad claimed that he "loved and worshipped" Patricia and that he felt hurt, disappointed, and confused by her negativity, lack of appreciation and understanding, and recent sexual withdrawal. He believed that he and Patricia were "the classic successful couple" and stated that he would do anything to make her happy. These statements made Patricia feel "crazy," and she wondered whether they "were even talking about the same marriage."

Brad's History with Patricia

The couple met when Patricia asked Brad for some advice at his nutritional supplement store. Patricia had hoped that Brad could recommend some supplements to correct the nutritional imbalance that she feared her bulimia might be causing. Brad recalled thinking that Patricia's eyes "were the color of amethyst" and that she was "absolutely stunning." He offered to place a special order for her, even though the supplements were in stock, just so he could get her phone number. Two days later, he dropped off the supplements at her house.

Patricia was an interior designer, and when Brad initially walked into her apartment, he was immediately impressed with her "relaxed yet elegant style." He gave her the supplements and asked about her bulimia. Hesitantly, Patricia talked about when her father, a physician, had died suddenly and left her mother overwhelmed by single parenthood. Attempting to minimize her mother's stress, Patricia had tried to be perfect, and somehow being thin became part of that quest for perfection. Brad remembers putting his arm around her and telling her that she was perfect already and how he hoped he could help her learn to see her perfection. Patricia wept, saying that she'd never opened up so much to someone before. At that moment of "complete and utter honesty," Brad fell in love with her.

Brad describes the first years of their marriage as "wonderful." He was always supportive, and Patricia had considered him "a great husband." Three years into their marriage, Patricia gave birth to a healthy baby girl and cut back on her design practice. Her reduced work hours, combined with Brad's support, reduced her tension and made her less prone to bulimic episodes.

From Brad's perspective, the next several years were "charmed." Their son was born, their daughter was "delightful," and Brad had been able to refer several of his wealthiest customers to Patricia for their remodeling projects. Additionally, Brad acquired the reputation among his customers of being a "better healer" than their physicians, which made his business flourish and allowed him to open a second store.

But Patricia had many concerns. Although she greatly respected Brad's clinical skills, she remembered hearing her father talk about complicated cases that had required referrals to specialists who could implement the latest scientific and technological discoveries. She worried that Brad's belief that he was a better healer than his customers' physicians was unrealistic and could lead to a customer's delaying or not receiving proper treatment, as well as to a potential lawsuit. Brad found her concerns insulting and refused to discuss them further.

Brad was also extremely competitive with others. Whether it was the front lawn, a new car, a vacation, or a computer, Brad needed the very latest and best, especially compared to what their neighbors and friends had. Once obtained, he disparaged those with less. Brad stated that he sought the very best only because his family deserved it and that he never wanted them to feel ashamed. But Patricia pointed out that Brad's compulsive buying was communicating warped values to the children, and had caused such financial strain that they'd needed the capital from Patricia's trust fund to avoid serious debt. She repeatedly asked to be included in decisions about major purchases and vacation plans, but Brad gave her request only lip service.

Brad's compulsion to compare—if not to compete—with others extended to bodies and appearance. A self-proclaimed "exercise fanatic," Brad talked about his own muscular development and that of others at the gym or of strangers on the street. If an obese person walked by, he quietly made disapproving remarks to Patricia about that person and questioned how he or she could live that way. These remarks troubled Patricia, not only for their lack of compassion but also because of her own recent weight gain.

Part of Patricia's weight gain was the healthy result of Brad's support in helping her overcome her bulimia. The rest of the weight gain was due to anxious eating and, in a contradictory way, her worry about Brad's opinion of her. If they were watching television and a pretty woman appeared on the screen, he'd comment on the woman's "beautiful body," which made Patricia feel ugly and fat. Brad clarified his comments by saying that he was simply making "an observation" and that he found Patricia's body quite sexy. He believed her "mis-interpretations" demonstrated her unhappiness with her size, which was why he reminded her to exercise, brought home books on nutrition, and made diet drinks for her. He was dumbfounded that these actions made Patricia feel bad.

Brad's unwillingness to empathize with Patricia was in sharp contrast to the empathic way he treated his dog. He worried that the dog might be too cold, too hot, too lonely, or ignored. The dog ruined Patricia's garden and wasn't properly housebroken, but Brad did little to control the dog's behavior. Tension developed with the neighbors, who'd called the police about the dog's barking. Brad thought the barking wasn't a problem and that their neighbors were being unreasonable, although Patricia agreed with the neighbors.

Not only did Patricia and Brad hold different opinions about events, they often recalled events differently, especially if the event involved Patricia's being the "hero." If Patricia had successfully dealt with an unhappy neighbor, an incorrect bill, or managing the children, Brad retold the event with himself as the hero. Even if Brad was the hero, in the retelling, his conquests took on proportions beyond what the reality had been.

The converse was also true: Brad never acknowledged making a mistake. If something was missing from Patricia's desk and later found on his, he'd simply shrug it off. If he'd committed to picking up Patricia at 5:30 but showed up at 6:00, he'd insist Patricia had given him the wrong time. Even when she showed him the e-mail stating 5:30, all he said was, "Oh." Brad was floored that these events meant so much to her. "Miscommunications happen," he explained, "but you've got to be more positive." Patricia felt that comments like this unfairly deflected the focus away from his error and onto her. Brad defended himself by stating that he wished she would appreciate what "a self-sacrificing, good man" he was and how hard he worked to make a positive difference in her life.

Patricia heartily agreed that he had made a positive difference in her life, but since he rarely, if ever, admitted any wrongdoing, she couldn't trust him. This lack of trust was especially troubling given her growing concerns about his marital fidelity, which had caused her to withdraw from him sexually. Two years ago, she had found a book of love poems in the glove compartment of his car inscribed in a feminine handwriting with "just because." Brad had explained that the book was nothing more than a gift from an appreciative customer.

The following year, just before Valentine's Day, Patricia saw Brad enter a lingerie shop and assumed he was buying her a present. When Valentine's Day arrived and Brad gave her candy, a gift she viewed as "insensitive" given her weight issue, she confronted him about the lingerie shop. Brad explained that he had planned to buy her something from the shop but that he couldn't find anything he thought she'd like in her size. Patricia took this explanation as another dig at her weight.

The final event that had aroused Patricia's suspicions had occurred a week prior to their seeking therapy. Brad had been waxing poetic about the "beauty and intelligence" of his chiropractor who was "fighting to maintain her self-esteem" while negotiating financial arrangements with her ex-husband. When Brad described how he had reassured the chiropractor that she was "perfect" and had offered to call her ex-husband to help, "an alarm went off" in Patricia's head, and she just knew they were having an affair.

Brad had denied Patricia's accusations and "refused to dignify them" by finding another chiropractor. He said that the store brought him into contact with a lot of women who, in the course of consulting him about their nutritional needs, revealed very personal and intimate information. He considered himself both good-looking and a good listener, a combination most women found attractive. And he believed that, after all these years, Patricia should have become used to it. He steadfastly maintained his denial that he had strayed. He added that he may have made decisions without her, but considering that he and Patricia "were so close," he naturally assumed that if his plans were good for him, they would be good for her. Most importantly, he was puzzled by and terribly hurt that all Patricia could focus on were "minor misunderstandings," when they enjoyed "such a great life together."

By the time he'd finished speaking, Patricia had started crying and said, "I've just said that you make me feel ugly and fat, that you never admit your mistakes, and that I suspect that you're having an affair, and you say we have a great life?" She turned to the therapist and asked, "Am I nuts to be upset?"

Brad's Previous Partners

Brad had always been very comfortable around women, and liked having many female friends. Prior to his relationship with Patricia, he'd had significant relationships with a rape survivor, an insomniac, and an unhappily married woman. These women had relied on Brad for help, and he'd felt "honored" that they had trusted him with their problems. However, he quickly clarified that what had attracted him to all of these women was not that their problems allowed him to "ride in on [his] white horse" but that he had "completely admired their incredibly strong characters."

Brad's Childhood and Early Adulthood

Brad was an only child, who grew up in the suburbs of a major city. His parents had met on a blind date, and they married ten months later, when his father was twenty-two and his mother was twenty. Brad believes his parents had a "great" marriage.

Brad describes his father as a "kind and good man" whose kindness led to people taking advantage of him. Brad's father had worked at a hardware store, and if someone had a need, whether that person was a customer, his wife, or his boss, Brad's father went out of his way to help. This helpful demeanor had caused him to neglect other responsibilities and delayed his promotion to manager, which kept him from achieving the stature that Brad believes he deserved. On the other hand, the owner of the hardware store recognized and appreciated his hard work, and helped him to obtain a very favorable home loan. As a result, his father was able to buy the nice house in the suburbs that Brad's mother had always wanted, even though it stretched the family's budget and required him to work overtime.

Overall, Brad put a positive spin on the events of his early life. He described his mother as a "remarkable and dedicated woman." She always assured him that he would become rich and famous by finding the cure for cancer, which Brad believes gave him the motivation to face intellectual challenges. She appreciated the importance of good self-esteem and had "never wanted [him] to feel like a failure." Brad remembers being six years old and worrying that he was stupid because he couldn't make the pieces of a jigsaw puzzle come together. He complained about it to his mother, who then swooped up the puzzle and announced that the puzzle was either defective or missing some crucial pieces.

When Brad started first grade, his mother developed frequent and severe episodes of abdominal pain. In spite of multiple visits to doctors, the cause of her pain remained unknown. These "attacks" forced her to stay home in bed, clutching a heating pad to her abdomen. Often, unknown to Brad's father or even against his wishes, Brad's mother called his school and told them Brad was sick, so he could stay home with her, watching TV, making up stories, and playing games. Brad remembered those days fondly. His mother would call him her "little doctor" because just having him near seemed to reduce her pain. Yet, at other times, she locked him out of her bedroom and yelled at him to leave her alone, or she sent him to school even when he was actually sick. Brad understands these events as indications of the severity of his mother's suffering.

When his mother wasn't sick, she had made sure that her son received all the accolades and recognition a child could obtain. When his homework or a school project hadn't received a top grade, his mother had marched into the principal's office insisting that Brad's work had been judged unfairly or incorrectly. His mother would explain that Brad's work was "more sophisticated" than that of the other students or that he had dealt with the topic in a more innovative or creative way than his "rigid" teacher could appreciate. Although this behavior would have embarrassed many children, Brad felt proud and protected by it. She was equally "protective" when the teacher complained that Brad spoke out of turn in class, had been rude to her and his classmates, and had called many class assignments "infantile and unnecessary."

"Infantile and unnecessary" had been his mother's response whenever his father had suggested setting a standard bedtime, allowance, or limits. Brad believed that his mother "recognized [his] ability to make good decisions," while his father was more "old school." Brad's mother always won the argument, and Brad credits his "inherently good judgment" to his mother's attitude. Not only did his mother allow him to set his own limits, as he got older, she sought his counsel on both trivial and nontrivial matters. She'd ask his opinions about a new car or a medical issue as casually as she'd ask him about her hair, makeup, or clothing, often overriding or ignoring his father's opinion.

Brad's mother had also ignored Brad's father's concerns about money and had refused to curtail her spending. Brad considers her a "visionary"; she could spot important trends and had appreciated the necessity of staying up-to-date and creating the best impression among their friends and neighbors. As a result, Brad always rode the best bicycle and watched the biggest television set. Brad had thoroughly enjoyed shopping with his mother. They got along "famously," and he still considers her his best friend.

Sometime around Brad's thirteenth birthday, his father was promoted to a position with greater status and a much higher salary. At that point, Brad's relationship with his mother lost its intensity. He attributed this to the fact that her illness had vanished, which had freed her to spend more nights and weekends away with her husband but had reduced her time with Brad. Nonetheless, Brad recalls being happy about her improved health and her ability to live a fuller life.

Also around Brad's thirteenth birthday, his grades went from outstanding to "very respectable," partly because he was distracted from studying by his various girlfriends' dramas and, in his sophomore year, by his relationship with a friend's mother. One day, Brad had dropped by to see his friend, only to discover his friend's attractive midthirties mother alone in the house, unhappy, and wearing only a towel from her shower. "Somehow" they'd ended up in bed together. This was Brad's first sexual experience. He never told his parents, and never considered this relationship either abusive or exploitative. He believes a real friendship developed between them that continued until the woman and her family moved away later that year.

Brad completed high school with a very respectable but not outstanding academic record. He was well liked in college and had many girlfriends, but his grades were not strong enough for medical school admission, much to his own and his mother's disappointment. Upon graduating from college, he got a job at a vitamin store and planned to retake the necessary science classes for admission to medical school and reapply. However, his job at the store required him to receive training about vitamins and health, subjects he found far more interesting than organic chemistry. The store he worked at quickly became one of the chain's most popular branches because of his ability to communicate with the customers about their various health issues. After several years of "making money for other people," Brad approached his father and his father's boss to discuss his options. Together, they loaned Brad start-up capital, which permitted him, at the age of twenty-nine, to open his own store. One year later, with his store flourishing and having regained his mother's respect, he met Patricia.

Understanding Brad

In several ways, Brad's childhood provided him with a very distorted, inflated, and unrealistic view of himself. His mother's adoration gave him the belief that he was above reproach. Yet the disparity between Brad's ideal self and his real self left him vulnerable to feeling shame. He handled his desperate need to keep feelings of shame and inadequacy out of his awareness by developing into a tarnished white knight. Repeatedly choosing women with significant problems allowed him "to ride in on [his] white horse" to be their rescuer and feel powerful. But his unwillingness to empathize, his tendency to distort, his need for perfection, and his wish for adoration ultimately led to conflict with his partner.

Mom's Special Boy

Looking superficially at little Brad with his mother, you might have thought how lucky they were to have such a good relationship. Indeed, Brad still regards his mother with respect and awe, and considers her to be supportive and protective, and his best friend. Although we certainly advocate supportive, protective, and loving parenting, Brad's mother's self-centered ideals placed an enormous burden on him: he was to find the cure for cancer, keep her abdominal pain away, and be the success her husband was not. His opinions on matters far beyond his comprehension were sought and followed, often overruling those of his father. In many ways his mother treated him like a partner. She asked his opinion about her hair and makeup, and, without his father's knowledge, kept him home from school to be with her.

We suspect that this overvaluation of Brad and undervaluation of her husband made Brad conflicted about his identification with his father, and fearful that his father was not strong. Yet needing to protect his internal image of his father, he emphasized what a "kind and good man" his father had been, and distorted his father's inability to take control by blaming others for his father's delayed professional success.

His mother's interventions with his elementary school prevented Brad from receiving a realistic appraisal of his work and behavior, and implied that being less than perfect was unacceptable and should be denied. The absence of rules and the overt communication that this young boy could do as he pleased only worsened the situation. But Brad also received other indications that his role as the perfect son was tenuous. The most dramatic indications occurred when Brad's mother locked him out of her bedroom or sent him to school sick. Thus, Brad's relationship with his mother was one of extremes—either completely attached or completely rejected.

It is interesting that Brad's sexual relationship with his friend's mother occurred shortly after his mother's illness abated and she became more interested in spending time with her husband. After having such an intense relationship with his mother, her withdrawal made Brad quite vulnerable and hence subject to becoming prey for his friend's mother's inappropriate and abusive behavior. Yet Brad, too shame-prone to have anything in his life be less than perfect or admit to any weakness, glorified this relationship, and by so doing made himself feel special and important.

Unwillingness to Empathize

Brad's unwillingness to be empathic led him to behave in a way that was toxic to his marriage. Praising the figure of another woman when he knew Patricia worried about her own weight and being unwilling to ever admit that he was wrong were behaviors that lacked empathy. Recognizing how his behavior had hurt Patricia would have involved seeing himself as fallible, which was an admission that Brad wouldn't allow himself to make, lest he experience shame and guilt. Brad was also unable to see that he and Patricia were separate individuals with different needs and desires. His denial of separateness reflected a very basic fear of being separate, and was an attempt to fill his sense of emptiness.

Needing to Idealize and Be Idealized

Both Patricia and Brad provided numerous examples of Brad's need to be seen as perfect: the positive spin he put on his difficult childhood, his denial of his wife's unhappiness, his compulsive need to acquire the best, and his tendency to make himself into a hero by distorting events. Brad's childhood had prevented him from developing an accurate perception of himself or his parents. It was too frightening to acknowledge that his parents were a disappointment, so he idealized them, especially his mother. Such idealization is hard to maintain, and it forced him to continually distort or deny reality to keep the discrepancy between his idealized and actual parents from his own awareness.

Brad also idealized his partners. Although his previous partners had all been troubled women, he described them as having "very strong characters." He emphasized their strengths and downplayed their troubles because of his need to see everything and everyone associated with him as perfect. This was especially apparent with Patricia. Because Brad did not differentiate between himself and his wife, if Patricia was perfect, then Brad was perfect. The same was true of his dog, who apparently could do no wrong.

Perhaps unable to handle another academic failure, Brad had chosen not to repeat the science classes he had needed for medical school admission. Giving up on medical school was a major break from his parents' view of their ideal son, and it had required him to distort his perception of himself and deny that he had disappointed them. Instead, he used the skills he had developed at his mother's bedside—reading people and helping them to cope with their physical ailments—to create a very successful store and become "a better healer" than their physicians. In this way, he had recovered from disappointing his parents and was able to feel proud of who he'd become, at least overtly.

In spite of his store's success, Brad's own need to be idealized was endless. His previous partners and Patricia all had difficulties that had made him feel strong, powerful, and, at least temporarily, adored. His need to be idealized easily drew him into a relationship with another woman, such as the chiropractor, a relationship in which he believed he would be highly valued. Whether or not they were actually having a sexual relationship, at the time of his initial therapy visit, he'd already idealized the chiropractor, noting her "beauty and intelligence" and thus increasing his own value with her interest in him.

The Impact on Patricia

Although we know little about Brad's impact on his previous partners, we do know that Patricia was very unhappy and quite confused about their marriage. Some of Brad's behavior had been helpful. Patricia credits her recovery from bulimia and her business success to Brad's support, both of which increased her self-esteem. However, other aspects of his helping behavior had hurt her. When he minimized her concerns, refused to take responsibility for his actions, claimed her "heroic" actions as his own, or left her out of decision making, he diminished her self-esteem. With Patricia's self-esteem lessened, Brad's own sense of security in the relationship increased, as she then relied on him to repair the very self-esteem that he had damaged.

■ Kimberly

Kimberly was a sophisticated, impeccably groomed, late-thirties art historian who managed an art gallery. Kimberly initially came into therapy after having been passed over for a promotion because she was not a "team player." This was not the first time Kimberly had received this kind of feedback, and she admitted that she had been "a little tense" at work. She blamed this tension on forty-five-year-old

Ben, her third husband, and his lack of appreciation for all she did in their marriage.

Kimberly's History with Ben

Seven years ago, Kimberly met Ben, a physics professor, at the local university's open house. At the time, she thought Ben was a "diamond in the rough," since he seemed to have no sense of fashion, food, wine, or anything remotely cultural but was extraordinarily kind and generous. Although obviously uncomfortable in social settings, he was a highly regarded academician, and his classes were always packed, due to his skill at making complex concepts accessible and interesting.

Although Kimberly had been raised in the heart of Manhattan culture with no shortage of money, Ben had grown up in a rural town with little money to cover the necessities. While Kimberly had dated frequently, Ben had dated very little in the five years following his first wife's death. In spite of, or perhaps because of, these differences, Ben was smitten by Kimberly, spilling his drink and stuttering as he tried to make conversation. Kimberly had found his awkwardness charming and quite different from the "smooth, overconfident" men she usually dated, and she suggested they meet for a drink the following night. Ben was so flustered and flattered by Kimberly's suggestion that when he couldn't find anything on which to write her number, he wrote it on his arm.

The next night, Kimberly and Ben met at a bar. Kimberly had loved how Ben was so attentive and yet hesitant around her, and she had felt sorry for him as he tried to discuss art history, an area he knew nothing about. By the end of the evening, Kimberly had found Ben so "endearing" that she had invited him up to her condo. The couple then started dating regularly and they were married six months later.

Amazed by her beauty and astonished that she wanted to be with him, Ben had put Kimberly on a pedestal. And Kimberly had set about her self-appointed "task" of introducing Ben to the finer things in life. Ben proved to be an apt pupil, casting aside his comfortable clothes for designer labels, dutifully reading the novels Kimberly thought were important, spending their money on fine wine and art, and giving up his chess club meetings to attend the opera, the ballet, or a society function.

In the bedroom as well, Kimberly gave Ben very specific instructions, which he happily followed. However, over the past two years, he had seemed preoccupied and less interested in Kimberly. He had suggested that they not attend Kimberly's functions all the time but go instead to one of his, and he became resentful when she refused. Several weeks later, Ben had announced that he would not be escorting Kimberly to an important society party but that he would attend an important faculty dinner instead, and he hoped that she would go with him. Kimberly, appalled by Ben's decision, asked an old boyfriend to escort her to her party.

Ben's change in his priorities had made Kimberly "testy," which, at one point, drove him to call her "controlling." Although Kimberly found Ben's remark hurtful, she patiently explained that given her background, she needed to make the choices so that they could avoid becoming "bourgeois couch potatoes." She also defended herself by reminding Ben that she had tried some of his favorite activities, like chess, but she knew nothing about the game and had thought it "boring."

One day, Ben joined Kimberly for her therapy session. Noting to the therapist that he still found Kimberly "stunning and intelligent," he questioned whether he could stay in their marriage. He acknowledged that after his first wife's death, he had become depressed and had led a very "monklike existence." Kimberly had brought him out of his shell and expanded his life, but her criticisms were now unbearable. There were occasions when she praised his assessment of a painting or his wine choice, but these intermittent compliments were overshadowed by her denigrations. Now he felt like a "prisoner and a fool."

Kimberly ruled the household, dictating the furniture, clothing, food, and entertainment choices. Anything he chose was automatically dismissed as lacking in sophistication and deemed unacceptable, be it a hotel, movie, or even, on one occasion, how to serve an artichoke. Perhaps what Ben found most troubling was that he no longer believed in himself, which was causing him to criticize or question his judgment about ordinary, mundane issues. Making a dinner reservation, buying something for his car, or even getting a haircut now sent him into a tailspin plagued by self-doubt about the "correctness" of his choice.

Additionally, Kimberly always had to be in the spotlight. Ben described a dinner party where the host and guests, all Kimberly's art-world friends, were interested in a physics concept. In his element, Ben gave an explanation that fascinated and entertained them. Yet as soon as he and Kimberly had returned home, she sullenly complained, "Did you have to be so entertaining? No one paid any attention to me!"

The last straw for Ben was Kimberly's frequent phone calls and ambiguous relationship with the ex-boyfriend who had escorted her to the society event. Since the party, the two often met to "talk about art." At that point in the joint-therapy meeting, Kimberly broke into Ben's litany and explained that her ex gave her an intellectual stimulation that Ben couldn't provide, a "fascinating understanding" of the interaction between art and society, and that Ben was behaving like "an insecure idiot." Ben found this offensive and asked for an apology. Kimberly thought for a moment and then begrudgingly said, "I'm sorry your feelings got hurt."

"It's not about my feelings," Ben quietly replied, "Its about your behavior."

"What?" she questioned. "You'd prefer to sit around some stinky, old apartment, eating frozen food and playing chess with a bunch of disgusting old men?"

Ben stared at the floor, looked from the therapist to Kimberly, and then left the office. Kimberly turned to her therapist and asked, "See what I mean? How can I possibly do well at work with this kind of attitude at home?"

Kimberly's Previous Partners

Kimberly didn't date in high school and had dated very little in college. After college, she had met her first husband, an "outstandingly creative" artist, in Paris. With his talent and her knowledge of the art world, she was sure they would be enormously successful—until he had drained their bank account to support his cocaine habit.

Her second husband was a "nationally recognized" theater critic whose emphasis on manners and culture had reminded her of her stepfather. After three years of what she had thought was a good marriage, he'd left her to pursue his romantic interest in a male actor. Upon reflecting on these two marriages and the relationships that had followed, she saw two consistent patterns: first, she had viewed all the men as exceptional in some way, either in terms of their intellect or their creativity; and second, all of these men had made her feel adored. Like Ben, initially, they had put her on a pedestal and, at least temporarily, had made her forget the insecurities of her childhood.

Kimberly's Childhood and Early Adulthood

Kimberly had been raised in Manhattan by her mother and step-father. Her mother, upon receiving her associate's degree in art from a community college in a small farming town, had moved to Manhattan, unrealistically planning to find work as an art critic. Instead, she had worked during the day as a personal assistant for a museum curator, and spent her evenings attending wild parties, doing drugs, and completely enjoying one type of Manhattan nightlife. This type of enjoyment had soon led to her pregnancy with Kimberly.

Kimberly's mother had been able to work throughout her pregnancy, and after giving birth, she brought Kimberly to work with her. When Kimberly was two years old, her mother became a personal assistant at a fine arts gallery owned by the man who would later become Kimberly's stepfather. At that time, Kimberly's stepfather was married and had a five-year-old son. Nonetheless, a year after her mother began working at the art gallery, he filed for divorce so that he could marry her mother.

Kimberly's stepbrother had taken on his rejected mother's fury and had directed his anger at his easiest target, Kimberly. Fortunately, her stepbrother visited only every other weekend, limiting the amount of time Kimberly was subjected to his tortures: name-calling, stealing or breaking her toys, hiding her special doll, punching, lying, and blaming.

The other difficult aspect of Kimberly's childhood was her mother's frequent absence from the home. When Kimberly asked her to stay home or questioned where she was going, her mother gave vague answers about meetings or charity work. Given her mother's late hours, these answers didn't make sense. Instead, Kimberly felt that her mother didn't value or want to be around her. With her mother spending so little time at home, Kimberly became quite close to her stepfather, whom she believes was also perplexed, confused, and hurt by her mother's lack of interest in their family. Indeed, Kimberly remembers worrying that her stepfather felt so lonely and unloved by her mother that he would seek a divorce. In Kimberly's mind, a divorce would have left her without any real parent or with a mother who needed parenting herself, so she did her best to compensate for her mother's absence.

Fortunately, she and her stepfather got along well. He taught her about art and culture, and emphasized the necessity of being "exceptional." But her stepfather was very particular in his definition of exceptional. Using the wrong fork, wearing a scarf that was too bright, or even exhibiting bad posture could bring on terse and disapproving remarks. Nonetheless, Kimberly had loved her life. They lived in a beautifully decorated apartment, and she enjoyed her ballet and art lessons. She did well in school, although her teachers believed that she spent too much time attending to inconsequential details because she was so fearful of making a mistake.

Sometime after Kimberly's ninth birthday, two events occurred that changed Kimberly's life. The first happened when her stepfather was taking her home from ballet class, and made an unannounced delivery of a small statue to a client. As their taxi pulled up to the client's building, they saw Kimberly's mother and the client in an amorous embrace. Kimberly's memory of the event is hazy, but she does recall that her mother had cried and her stepfather had shouted, throwing the statue at her mother and then jumping into the taxi and yelling to the driver, "Just go!"

After that incident, the atmosphere in the home changed. Kimberly's mother was rarely home, and when she was, she was often drunk. Her parents slept in separate bedrooms. Kimberly would stay awake until her mother had returned, and then quietly slip into her mother's bedroom and beg her to stay home and be nice to her stepfather. Her mother typically responded by calling her husband an "uptight asshole" who didn't know how to have a "good time" and thought himself "so exceptional." She believed that by marrying him, she had provided Kimberly with "one hell of a life," thereby fulfilling her responsibilities as a mother. Moreover, Kimberly "ought to be damned grateful for [her] sacrifice." Kimberly was especially hurt one evening when her mother shoved her out of her bedroom and yelled, "Stop being his little mouthpiece!"

Her stepfather was equally vocal in disparaging his wife. He called her a "slut from the sticks," and made many humiliating remarks, regardless of who was around or who might be hurt. At several parties, after drinking excessively, he introduced Kimberly as "my wife's souvenir from her partying days." When her mother was out at night, he seemed to focus only on Kimberly's mistakes, often blaming them on her "unknown genetic background." Still, Kimberly did her best to please him and obtain his approval. She dressed and spoke in the style he liked, ate with impeccable manners, and learned all she could about art in order to successfully answer his questions and converse with him.

The second significant event in Kimberly's childhood occurred when she was in the tenth grade. Kimberly's stepbrother, after being expelled from his school, had transferred to Kimberly's school for his senior year. Her stepbrother was a very troubled teenager who sold drugs and delighted in making inappropriate and derogatory sexual remarks to her and her mother on his weekend visits. Kimberly learned from her classmates that her stepbrother had repeated these remarks at school and had even told her classmates that he had seen her mother in a bar kissing another man.

Kimberly had tried to talk to her mother about her stepbrother's behavior and allegations, but her mother had just said to ignore him because they needed to keep the peace in their home. Much to Kimberly's dismay, her mother never denied that she was again having an affair.

After her stepbrother graduated, he left home for an out-of-state college. With her stepbrother out of the picture, Kimberly had hoped that her remaining years in high school would be free of the embarrassment he had created, but this was not to be. His vicious rumors had taken on a life of their own, and Kimberly found herself the subject of daily gossip and the object of cruel jokes. She recalled handling this shame by becoming ultrapolished in her dress, manner, and speech, and being overtly critical of other students who didn't meet her standards. This left her with an elite and very small group of girls who could be her friends.

Things were equally difficult at home. Her parents no longer spoke to each other, and her mother was sometimes gone for several days without an explanation. Kimberly pleaded with her mother to stay home, but her pleas fell on deaf ears. Eventually, she gave up and simply did her best to ignore her mother in the same manner that her mother was ignoring her.

As miserable as this life sounds, Kimberly recalled a positive side. Her stepfather needed a companion for his social functions, but her mother was unavailable and could not be counted on to behave appropriately. In contrast, Kimberly, in her quest to please her stepfather and keep herself socially above her gossiping classmates, was able to converse about art, books, and current events with a poise and maturity well beyond her years. Consequently, when she turned fifteen, her stepfather made Kimberly his escort for various social functions, preferring her youthful and compliant company to the potential embarrassment of his wife's behavior.

These functions were some of the happiest times of her life. Frequently, she was the youngest person at the event, and she loved the attention and praise she received. She felt special meeting well-known people and wearing the beautiful clothes her stepfather had selected for her. On their way home from these events, her stepfather would critique Kimberly's performance, usually positively. These positive critiques had a shameful side as well, such as when he'd praise himself for having successfully taught her how to overcome and keep hidden her "unknown heritage."

Upon graduating from high school, she attended an Ivy League college, where she studied art history, anticipating that she would work in her stepfather's gallery. However, shortly after she left for college, her stepfather developed health problems and sold the gallery. After graduating, Kimberly moved to Paris, worked in an art gallery there, and married. Several years later, when her first marriage failed, she left Paris to help run a gallery in the United States.

Understanding Kimberly

The material possessions in Kimberly's childhood did little to help her cope with her basic sense of inadequacy and her fear that her flaws would be revealed. She obtained a false sense of security by finding partners who made her feel adored yet still had a need or trait that gave her control, such as Ben's social awkwardness. Her unconscious hope was that the relationship would heal or cover over the feelings of insecurity and inadequacy she had developed in childhood, and that it would repair her self-esteem.

However, as is sadly typical of many tarnished white knights, the sense of emptiness, the emotional hole that she hoped a partner could fill remained painfully present. Consequently, although Kimberly initially idealized Ben, ultimately she devalued him and refused to accept any responsibility for their failing marriage.

Kimberly's Sources of Shame

Before and after Kimberley's birth, her mother's behavior was a very sad embarrassment, and as a young child Kimberly took on her mother's shame. Her mother had had an unwanted pregnancy, was an alcoholic, had emotionally abandoned Kimberly, and had been disloyal to her husband, if not sexually promiscuous. As a young child, Kimberly's stepbrother, perhaps dealing with his anger at being abandoned by his father, had made Kimberly the target of his rage. In high school, he had created and perpetuated ugly rumors and gossip about her and her mother. Although Kimberly had become quite attached to her stepfather, it was at a cost to her self-esteem, because she had taken all of his criticisms to heart.

Stepfather's Special Girl

With her mother neither present nor an appropriate role model, Kimberly had looked to her stepfather for parenting, and he had taken on the role eagerly. Viewing her as an extension of himself, he needed to make Kimberly the perfect young lady in dress, manner, and cultural sophistication. But any failure on her part, such as using the wrong fork or wearing too bright a scarf, led him to remind her that at a level as basic as her DNA, she was inadequate: her paternity was unknown and assumed to be deficient, and her mother was, at best, inappropriate.

Regardless of how cultured Kimberly may have appeared on the outside, at her core she identified with her mother and felt terribly flawed. All of her attempts to have her mother behave more like a parent had failed. Her stepfather was all she had, and she feared she could lose him as she had emotionally lost her mother. Her mother's remark that Kimberly was her stepfather's "mouthpiece" had contained an element of truth. Out of necessity, Kimberly had idealized him, and it was her stepfather, not her mother, who had her loyalty.

Consequently, Kimberly did the best she could to keep him in her life, believing that if this idealized, cultured man loved her, then she could be someone other than her defective mother's daughter. This idealization had made his criticism even more devastating.

Although Kimberly's efforts were successful and she was rewarded with the heady experience of being her stepfather's escort, she continued to struggle with being emotionally abandoned by her mother and basically flawed. In spite of the glamour of being her stepfather's escort, his constant evaluation of her appearance and conduct at the events they attended, and his references to her flawed genetics had only added to her feelings of inadequacy.

Dealing with Feelings of Inadequacy

As a child, Kimberly's need to cover her feelings of inadequacy had taken the form of anxiously spending an inordinate amount of time on her schoolwork to make it perfect, often to her own detriment. As a teenager, she had coped with the shame about her identity, her stepfather's criticism, her mother's behavior, and her stepbrother's humiliating revelations by becoming overtly contemptuous and critical of the dress, manners, and sophistication of most of her classmates.

Although such critiques can be a part of high-school relationships, Kimberly's excessive contempt and her high standards made her difficult to be around, and as a result, she had few friends. This behavior was, in part, an identification with her stepfather. Just as he had criticized her, she criticized others. It was also an attempt to rid herself of her own shame about being unworthy and inadequate. That is, by focusing attention on the weaknesses of others, Kimberly's own shame could remain hidden from herself and her friends.

As an adult, one of the ways Kimberly protected herself from her sense of inadequacy was by idealizing and devaluing her partners. Ben and her two previous husbands were "exceptional," not unlike what her stepfather had expected from her. Her first husband was "outstandingly creative," her second husband was "nationally recognized," and Ben was a "highly regarded" academician. Most importantly, they had made her feel adored, and by idealizing them she had increased her own value. But ultimately, when she sensed rejection, she devalued Ben in order to diminish his power and her own feelings of loss.

Kimberly was extremely controlling with Ben. This control repeated the culture lessons she had received from her stepfather, only now she was the teacher and Ben was the flawed and inadequate student. Her controlling behavior also protected her from having her own inadequacy exposed, and it made her feel powerful. Deciding on the menu, the furnishings, and their activities kept her away from new situations where her weakness might have been revealed, such as at Ben's faculty party.

Even within her own circle of friends, she couldn't always be in control or the center of attention. As a teenager, being her stepfather's escort had inflated her feelings of self-worth, temporarily helped her put aside her fears of inadequacy, and hid her envy of others. As an adult, she still needed experiences that bolstered her sense of self. Thus, when Ben was the star of the dinner party, Kimberly was unable to tolerate the lack of attention, and became sullen.

The Impact on Ben

Unable to recognize her own shortcomings at work or in her marriage, Kimberly was a difficult partner. Her fragile self-esteem made it impossible for her to take responsibility or apologize for anything, lest she feel shamed at her exposed weakness. She even blamed Ben when she wasn't promoted, minimizing her employer's feedback that she was not a "team player." Her recent ambiguous relationship with her ex-boyfriend was another way in which she controlled Ben. By making Ben feel jealous and insecure, she could deny her own feelings of insecurity and vulnerability, and reset the power dynamic within their relationship.

In this atmosphere, Ben found himself plagued by self-doubt. Having taken on Kimberly's insecurity and fear of inadequacy, he now questioned his judgment and feared embarrassment over insignificant decisions. His depression following his first wife's death had made him lack social confidence and, at least temporarily, view Kimberly as helpful. He readily agreed that with Kimberly's encouragement and confidence, he was enjoying a more active social life. But over time, her unwillingness to empathize with or recognize the hurt she caused him became unacceptable. Almost as a matter of survival, Ben was on his way out of the marriage.

Tarnished Patterns

Both Brad and Kimberly needed to take measures to reconcile the disparities between their real and ideal selves, and to keep their vulnerabilities hidden from their own and others' awareness. As a result, they found partners with a tangible trait or situation that required rescue. Brad and Kimberly desperately hoped that by rescuing their partners, they would receive the validation they had lacked in their childhoods.

The Cost of Being Special

Brad's mother and Kimberly's stepfather had communicated that Brad and Kimberly were expected to achieve a level of perfection that doomed them both to failure. Their parents' unrealistic expectations and unattainable ideals had led Brad and Kimberly to feel that they were flawed, inadequate, and disappointing. Consequently, each of them developed emotionally costly measures to keep their real or imagined inadequacies from being seen.

On a daily basis, Brad had to live up to his mother's belief that he was special and above reproach. When his presence failed to relieve her pain or when she was just in a bad mood and sent him to school sick, she communicated the instability of her dedication to him. As a young adult, when he failed to be accepted to medical school, he had needed to take measures to cope with disappointing his parents and himself. Kimberly had to cope with her stepfather's ideal of being exceptional, while at the same time being told that at her core she was inadequate. As adults, both Kimberly and Brad handled their parents' inevitable disappointment by finding a partner in need of rescuing, and then making their partners feel the shame they themselves had felt as children.

Picking a Partner

Brad's previous partners had all been women with significant current or past challenges. Patricia's bulimia was especially compelling, because it allowed him another chance at "curing" the important woman in his life and repairing the damage to his self-esteem that remained from having failed to "cure" his mother. Kimberly's husbands were all "exceptional," as though she were still trying to please her stepfather by her choice of partner. However, her first husband had also had a substance abuse problem, just like her mother.

Ben needed rescuing from his social awkwardness and depression. Although Kimberly's mother had not been socially isolated, her alcoholism suggests that she, like Ben, may have suffered from depression. When Kimberly behaved like her stepfather and took control of her life with Ben, she was trying to rescue Ben from his depression in the same way that she had tried to rescue her mother. Thus as children, Kimberly and Brad had both failed to rescue their needy parents. As adults, by picking partners in need of similar rescuing, they provided themselves with another chance to be a successful rescuer and the hope of getting what they had not received in childhood: the empathy, attunement, and validation that would give them a more secure sense of self.

Rescuing Behavior and Results

Brad and Kimberly were successful in rescuing their current partners from their initial perils. Patricia's bulimia abated thanks to Brad's support, and Ben became more socially comfortable thanks to Kimberly's encouragement to be social and outgoing. Yet Brad's and Kimberly's overt and covert criticisms of their partners, delivered under the guise of rescuing, eventually damaged their partners' self-esteem, similar to the way in which Brad and Kimberly felt damaged.

Additionally, by making their partners jealous—Brad, by his ambiguous relationship with his chiropractor, and Kimberly, by her ambiguous relationship with her ex-boyfriend—they kept themselves powerful in their primary relationships by evoking insecurity in their partners. As a result, Brad and Kimberly both maintained their positions as rescuers who could now rescue their partners from the very insecurity they had caused their partners to feel.

Trapped by Shame

Failing to achieve their impossible ideals caused Brad and Kimberly to feel shame. This shame trapped them in various unhealthy self-protective behaviors that ultimately ruined their relationships. One way that Brad and Kimberly dealt with their sense of failure was through their grandiosity, seeing themselves as extremely successful and competent—and in many ways they were.

However, their grandiosity and arrogance prevented a realistic self-assessment, which put them at risk in their work and intimate relationships. For example, Brad coped with his parents' and his own disappointment that he had not gone to medical school by believing that he was "a better healer" than a physician. Kimberly coped with her inevitable failure at being her step-father's perfectly cultured daughter by seeing herself as the purveyor of culture in her relationship with Ben. Trying to hide the imperfections they felt on the inside, they sought to surround themselves with perfection on the outside: their homes, possessions, partners, or their own behavior. When reality interfered with their belief in their own perfection, they distorted reality or became highly critical of others, often their partners, so as to keep their own failings out their own awareness.

Summing Up

The tarnished white knight finds a partner she can rescue to keep her own sense of inadequacy hidden. Her rescuing includes behaviors that may be helpful, but she can also be emotionally destructive to her partner. Fearing her own imperfection, she distorts events or her own or the other's qualities so as to maintain the image of herself as infallible. She refuses to take responsibility for her actions, is critical of her partner, and is unwilling to empathize with him, thereby evoking in him the very feelings of inadequacy that exist within herself. As a result of these self-protective maneuvers, her partner often ends up feeling humiliated and wanting to leave the relationship.

In chapter 7, you will see how the need to keep his sense of inadequacy hidden also influences the rescuing behavior of the terrorizing/terrified white knight but in a more terrifying manner.

Thinking About It

- Are you able to admit your mistakes without trying to equalize the situation by negatively commenting on your partner's behavior?

- How do you feel at a party or social gathering when someone else is the center of attention?

- Are you able to try something new that may be challenging for you but that your partner will enjoy?

- Has your partner complained that he wants an equal say in decisions affecting both of you, such as major purchases, vacations, housing, and so forth?

- Were your caregivers' expectations for you realistic?

7

Knight Stories: The Terrorizing/Terrified White Knight

The terrorizing/terrified white knight struggles to keep her vulnerability hidden. Her reactions to shame and weakness are more intense than those of the tarnished white knight. Given her chaotic inner world, she believes she must take extreme measures to maintain a sense of emotional safety, stay close to her partner, and avoid abandonment. These measures often involve physically and emotionally controlling her partner.

Needing to keep his fear and shame hidden from others, the terrorizing/terrified white knight is reluctant to risk exposure by participating in psychotherapy. If he does go for treatment, it is usually at the insistence of some external source: a partner who is threatening to leave or an outside agency, legal or otherwise, that requires him to be in therapy.

Brenda, the first terrorizing/terrified white knight we discuss in this chapter, was motivated to seek treatment because her boyfriend had threatened to leave her if she didn't seek help. The external motivating source for Victor, the second terrorizing/terrified white knight we discuss, was his son's residential treatment facility's requirement that all parents had to participate in couples therapy. In spite of their very different life experiences, both of these white knights continually found partners who needed rescuing, but sadly, their own internal terror drove them to rescue their partners in a terrifying manner.

■ Brenda

Dressed younger than was appropriate for her forty-six years, Brenda came for therapy with Tony, her twenty-nine-year-old, live-in boyfriend. Brenda owned a commercial real estate firm, where she had hired Tony as the office manager. Tony was threatening to leave their five-year relationship unless she demonstrated a sincere and effective effort in curtailing her explosive temper, and allowed him to have "a life." In her most recent temper outburst, Brenda had thrown Tony's personal digital assistant (PDA) out the window of her moving automobile. When it hit the pavement, it had bounced onto an oncoming car and shattered the windshield.

Fortunately, no one was hurt, but the owner of the other vehicle had called the police. Brenda told the police officer that it had been an accident and that she would gladly pay the damages. Tony, knowing that Brenda had received prior citations and not wanting Brenda to be arrested, supported her story. Brenda felt that Tony was blackmailing her to go for therapy and that the only reason she was "wasting time and money on therapy" was because Tony refused to have sex with her, and he was sleeping in a separate room.

Brenda's History with Tony

Brenda had met Tony at the racetrack. The horses weren't running for Tony that day, and he was down a substantial amount of money. Brenda, who loved gambling on the horses and went to the track several times a year, had quickly seen the error in Tony's betting strategy. Under her guidance, Tony soon recouped his losses and more. In appreciation, he'd bought Brenda a drink at a nearby bar.

Over drinks, Brenda learned that when Tony was eighteen he had been incarcerated on a "bogus" drug trafficking charge. After spending two years in a minimum security prison, he had been cleared of all charges but he had continued to live "on the edge." For the past four years, he had drifted in and out of various jobs, unable to find a career that suited him. He had come to the track hoping to win enough money to allow him to pay off debts, and then find his passion.

When Brenda met Tony, she had recently ended a relationship with a married man and was "needing some real male company." She recalled thinking that Tony was exceptionally attractive; had a sexy, easygoing manner; and was young and hence malleable. She invited him to her home, and at the end of the weekend, which they both described as a "sexual marathon," she suggested that he move in with her. Tony hesitated, fearing the relationship was moving too fast. But Brenda argued that she knew a "good horse" when she saw one, and cited her success at the track as proof. Three weeks later, Tony moved into Brenda's home.

Tired of managing her incompetent office manager, Brenda fired him and trained Tony to take over. Brenda's financial skill, combined with Tony's good looks and affable manners, was a winning ticket for their bank account. So confident was Brenda that she mapped out a financial plan that would allow them both to retire in seven years.

The couple seemed to get along well, working hard during the day and enjoying drugs, sex, and partying at night. On their weekends, Brenda involved Tony in her volunteer work for a nearby farm for retired racehorses. Their first major altercation occurred one year into their relationship, when Brenda was to meet Tony at a bar after work. She arrived early, and before Tony saw her, she saw him "cooing and preening over some twenty-two-year-old." Brenda discreetly sat down off to the side and ordered two martinis. She drank the first, and then carried the second to Tony's table and poured it onto his lap. Then she picked up the younger woman's drink and threw it in her face, called her "a whore," and stormed out.

When Tony came home later that evening, he explained that the young woman was an old friend and that Brenda had completely misinterpreted the situation. What had troubled him more was what he'd learned from a man who witnessed Brenda's outburst. The man had identified himself as a good friend of Brenda's previous romantic partner, the married man. Brenda had always been evasive when Tony had asked about that relationship. From the man he'd met in the bar, Tony learned that Brenda had smashed eggs on the married man's car, left threatening notes, called the married man's boss about an alleged embezzlement, and made late-night anonymous phone calls to his wife.

Flying into a rage that Tony believed "those lies," Brenda had smashed all the dishes on the floor, making so much noise that the neighbors called the police. When the police arrived, Tony assured them that Brenda had simply tripped while carrying a tray of dishes.

After several days of silence, Brenda made Tony swear on his mother's soul that he didn't believe what the man in the bar had told him.

Several months went by without incident, but Tony was becoming restless. He decided to complete his bachelor's degree, so he asked Brenda for money to attend a local private college. Initially, Brenda refused, stating that the money would take them "off plan," and questioned his need for a degree. Tony argued that a degree would allow him to be "[his] own person" and not be dependent upon Brenda forever. He also argued that the thousands of dollars Brenda contributed every year to support retired racehorses could be used instead for his education without having any impact on their bottom line.

Brenda became furious. She thought that Tony was mocking her dedication to the horses and that he did not understand the importance of her charitable work. But mostly she feared that his request was a precursor to his leaving her. Tony did his best to assure her otherwise, but Brenda wouldn't give in until Tony withdrew emotionally and sexually. Eventually, just to "make him happy," she agreed to his attending a part-time night school. Although this was certainly a different conclusion than what he had sought, he was grateful for all that Brenda provided, and resumed their sexual intimacy.

Tony's schooling didn't go well. Brenda objected to him being away two nights a week, meeting with his classmates, or his focus on his studies when she wanted to "party." She feared that he was seeing "some young chick," and asked detailed questions about his activities, trying to find inconsistencies. A few times she showed up unexpectedly at his classroom, allegedly to drive him home. She issued an edict that he was not to spend time with the other young men in his classes because all they wanted to do was to pick up girls. Nor was he allowed to meet his female classmates about their joint class project, unless they met at Brenda's house.

On the one occasion when a female classmate came to the house to work on a project, Brenda had "sashayed about" in suggestive clothing, touched Tony in overtly sexual ways, and offered the young woman cocaine for a potential threesome. The embarrassed classmate had quickly left. Tony, incensed and humiliated by Brenda's behavior, accused Brenda of ruining his life. Brenda, outraged that Tony should criticize her while defending his classmate's abrupt departure, punched Tony and gave him a black eye. His injury startled her, and she became terrified that Tony would leave. To make amends, she withdrew her restrictions and said that Tony could meet his classmates at the library. However, this particular student, as well as the other young women in the class, no longer wanted anything to do with Tony.

Later in the school year, another class had required a joint project. This time, Tony teamed up with a male classmate and, as agreed to by Brenda, met his partner at the library. However, after their third meeting, Tony came home to discover Brenda dancing in their living room with a man she'd met that night at a bar. After a brief altercation, Tony kicked the man out of the house. Interestingly, both Tony and Brenda recall that night as one of their most intense and passionate sexual encounters.

In spite of these difficulties, Tony completed his bachelor's degree in accounting. Brenda had hoped that with his having "gotten the education thing out of his system," life could proceed as she had planned. But one of Tony's teachers had recommended him for a job as an auditor at a local financial company, and Tony was eager and excited to make a good salary on his own. Anticipating Brenda's negative reaction, Tony had not told her about the opportunity until after the company had told him that he was a serious candidate.

Much to Tony's surprise, rather than exploding, Brenda had smiled and simply said, "Congratulations, sweetheart. I'm very proud of you." Two days later, Tony received an e-mail from the company that said he was no longer being considered. Very upset by this unexpected turn of events, Tony had e-mailed the teacher, asking him to find out what happened. Several days later, while Brenda was driving them home, Tony received a message on his PDA from the teacher, who had learned that Tony had been dropped from consideration because of his "questionable and previously undisclosed history of incarceration." Furious, Tony had accused Brenda of contacting the company. Brenda denied the charge and became so angered by the accusation that she grabbed his PDA and hurled it out of the car window.

In therapy, Brenda described herself as a "passionate for life" person who "feels things intensely." She did say that if she had hurt him, she was sorry, but she wished that he would try to understand her better. She added that it was her passion that had caused her to react so intensely when Tony withdrew sexually, emotionally, or strayed from her plan. She also maintained her denial of having contacted his potential employer or of having committed any malicious acts against the married man.

Brenda's Previous Relationships

Brenda had a very active romantic and sexual life prior to meeting Tony. She claimed she just "liked sex" and that she wasn't bothered by one-night stands. She wanted to be in control, and freely admitted that she'd generally dated men whom she could control. After two failed marriages, she'd promised herself she would never marry again. Her first marriage had been to a wealthy real estate investor, twenty years her senior, whom she'd met while he was still married to another woman. He and his wife were no longer sexual because he suffered from impotence. After secretly dating Brenda, his impotence problem had vanished, so he'd divorced his wife and married Brenda. Several years and smashed television sets later, his sexual dysfunction returned. He had confessed that he found Brenda "frightening," and said that he could no longer live with her.

Her second husband had also been a real estate investor, and he was fourteen years older than Brenda. Although he had no sexual problems, his temper was every bit as volatile as hers. Rather than simply tolerate her outbursts, he'd fought back, and Brenda had found herself frightened, as frightened as she had been as a child.

After Brenda's second divorce, all of the men she dated had been at least ten years younger than she. This was no coincidence. Thinking that she could train a younger man to be more to her liking, she had actively sought them out. Her relationship prior to Tony had been with a married man twelve years her junior. Brenda had helped him to pay off his debts, taken him on expensive vacations, and given him money for a divorce attorney. After two years of no movement on the divorce and upon learning that her married lover's wife was pregnant, Brenda had broken off the relationship. In spite of this unhappy ending, Brenda continued to maintain her belief that younger men were more appreciative of her and what she could do for them. Moreover, they made her feel sexy, desirable, and secure.

Brenda's Childhood and Early Adulthood

Brenda's parents met when her mother was eighteen and working as a receptionist at the loan company where Brenda's father, then thirty-three years old, worked as an agent. Shortly after her parents had met, her mother had become pregnant with Brenda's older brother, and her parents had married. Brenda was born fifteen months after her older brother, and her mother never went back to work. Her father left the loan company, which he'd always described as a "dead end," to establish his own company. Brenda's understanding of how her father made a living is vague. However, what she does recall suggests that he dealt in real estate foreclosures, acting as a middleman, and often in "shady deals."

Brenda jokingly describes her childhood as filled with "the good, the bad, and the ugly." She enjoyed playing sports with her brother, and was surprisingly good at baseball. Both Brenda and her father loved horses and going to the racetrack. Although her age prevented her from actually betting, her father had taught her how to interpret the *Daily Racing Form*, figure out the odds, strategically manage her money, and—what Brenda had loved the most—how to judge and observe the horses. Often before a race, her father talked to one of the trainers, ostensibly so that Brenda could be close to the horses. She later realized that her father had been getting inside information.

But there had also been plenty of very bad and ugly times. Brenda's parents had fought frequently, mostly about gambling and other women. Typically, Brenda was awakened by her father returning home late at night when her mother screamed at him for spending their money on his "whores." As Brenda and her brother grew older, they had tried to mediate to keep the peace.

Brenda's most terrifying memory involves a night when her mother was drunk and wielding a kitchen knife. As her parents wrestled for possession of the knife, Brenda's brother, who was thirteen at the time, burst down the stairs and threw himself at their parents. Her father pushed him away and inadvertently into a bookcase. The bookcase toppled over onto the boy, knocking him out and breaking his arm. Frightened by the sight of their unconscious and injured son, her parents had stopped fighting and tried to revive him. When the ambulance arrived, her mother told the paramedics that the bookcase had fallen when the children accidentally bumped into it during their roughhousing.

The bookcase incident seemed to shock her parents into behaving more appropriately toward each other, at least temporarily, but it was still not a happy home. Brenda's older brother spent very little time there, hating his father and feeling betrayed by his mother for lying about the bookcase. Shortly after the bookcase incident, he abandoned his sports friends for a group of boys her father described as "hoodlums." Although her father began coming home at an appropriate hour, he seemed moody, and he focused almost exclusively on his work.

Brenda's life was further complicated by her mother's belief that her father had not stopped seeing other women but that he had simply become more skilled at hiding his affairs. Brenda became her mother's reluctant companion and helper in the search for "the truth." This search included helping her mother pick the lock on her father's filing cabinet, steaming open his mail, making anonymous phone calls to verify his whereabouts, and inquiring about suspicious credit card charges.

Her mother had insisted that Brenda do the investigating, believing that if her father ever found out that Brenda's mother was spying on him, he would kill her. Brenda was "Daddy's little princess," so her mother assumed that she would be immune from his wrath. Brenda remembered his wrath and wasn't convinced of her immunity; however, she was certain that her father was innocent, and she hoped that, with enough evidence, her mother would feel secure. Finally, when Brenda was thirteen, after accompanying her mother on a fruitless stakeout, which had caused Brenda to miss another party, Brenda had refused to participate any further. This made her mother so furious that she slapped Brenda across the face.

Following that incident, Brenda and her mother rarely spoke. One day, Brenda came home and found her mother sitting quietly at the table. She looked at Brenda and softly said, "Your son-of-a-bitch father has gone and left us to marry his whore. Are you happy now?" Brenda didn't see or hear from her father for several years. Later, he tracked her down to introduce her to her new stepmother.

Looking back, Brenda wonders whether her father's abrupt departure played a role in her own behavior change. In elementary school, she was very shy, but as she got older, she became "sneaky" and skilled at lying. She'd successfully lie to her teachers about her missing homework or why she was late for class, and she paid or intimidated her classmates into letting her copy their exams. She made the girls' varsity softball team but was eventually thrown off the team for cheating and unsportsmanlike conduct toward her teammates, the umpire, and the other teams.

After graduating from high school, nothing held Brenda to her hometown. By then, her brother was working on an oil rig, her relationship with her mother was filled with anger, and she had few friends because of her temper and manipulative behavior. She knew a fair amount about real estate and finance from listening to her father, and she found a job as an assistant in a real estate firm three hours away. Fifteen years later, thanks to her ruthlessness and having wisely invested the divorce money she received from her first husband, she owned her own company.

Understanding Brenda

Brenda's early emotional life had been riddled with terror, shame, and rage. The tremendous fear generated by witnessing her parents' battles had left her with deep emotional scars that played out in her adult relationships. She had tried to create security for herself and to escape from her emotions by controlling her partners with her volatile temper and use of humiliation. Such behaviors are characteristic of terrorizing/terrified white knights.

A Terrorizing/Terrified Family

Except for the one time her mother had slapped her across the face, Brenda was never physically abused. Nonetheless, her parents' frequent and vicious fights had placed her in a terrifying environment. Having parents who were so out of control so often meant that she never felt safe and secure: if her parents could treat each other viciously, they might treat her viciously as well. She had been a pawn in her parents' relationship and had taken on their adult issues, such as the role of sleuth for her mother or as a racetrack foil for her father, and she was made to feel responsible for her father's departure.

Brenda's Identifications

Neither of Brenda's parents had been good role models, yet they were all she had for guidance and example. In some ways, she saw her father as the stronger of the two parents, and she identified with many of his characteristics. She was skilled with money, and used his gambling principles as guidelines for successfully managing her finances. He had been involved in real estate, albeit a "shady" aspect of real estate, but it was still an area in which Brenda had developed an expertise. Perhaps the most positive identification she had with him was his love of the racetrack, which had given Brenda many warm memories and encouraged her love of horses. Indeed, it was only with retired racehorses that she felt emotionally safe enough to be compassionate and empathic.

Brenda also identified with her parents' negative qualities. Her father lied to his wife, most likely lied to his clients, and had cheated at the racetrack.

Brenda adopted his use of deception, fraudulence, hostility, and devious conduct, as well as her mother's suspicious nature, fear of abandonment, and lack of control. As an adolescent and after her father had left, she manipulated, cheated, and lied. As an adult, she did whatever she felt was necessary, regardless of its legality or morality, to have her needs met.

When her father left her mother for another woman, Brenda was abandoned as well. Her mother had tried to manage her own fear of being abandoned by investigating his fidelity, hoping that more information would give her a greater sense of control. And just as her mother had spied on and stalked her father, Brenda relentlessly questioned Tony and unexpectedly showed up at his classes. When Brenda saw Tony at the bar with a young woman, her buried feelings were triggered. She immediately saw herself abandoned, as her mother had been, and she lost control.

Picking a Partner

Ultimately, all of Brenda's significant relationships paralleled the relationship between her parents. Brenda's first two husbands were wealthy real estate investors and could have been seen as successful versions of her father. After her marriages to these two older men failed, Brenda had made a decision to limit her relationships to dependent younger men, whom she could mold into the partners she wanted. However, this choice may have represented an unconscious shift in her identifications. Rather than being like her mother in the relationship—younger, dependent, vulnerable, and eventually abandoned—Brenda chose to be like her father: older, wiser, independent, and ostensibly in charge. Although her relationship with a younger married man immediately prior to her relationship with Tony had failed, Tony had seemed perfect. He had no ties to his family and no real source of income. When he began to pursue a college education, she felt him slipping out of her control.

Anger and Control

Having adopted her frightening early childhood experience as a prototype for her life, Brenda mistakenly believed that she could control her sense of security by controlling her partner. Instead of trying to be the best, most loving, and supportive partner she could be, she did all she could to control Tony and to maintain his dependence on her. She issued edicts, made unreasonable demands, and humiliated him. It is no wonder that Tony believed she had betrayed his confidence in order to sabotage his job opportunity. In the end, her controlling behavior put her in the unsettling position of not knowing why Tony was really with her: did he love her or need her, or was it that he simply couldn't escape her control?

As much as Brenda controlled others in her efforts to keep them close, she was unable to control herself and her rage. Overlapping sources contributed to her rage. The first was her fear that she would be hurt or abandoned. When this fear was triggered, she became overwhelmed, panicked, and reverted back to her early identifications with her disturbed parents, reflexively reacting in a similarly violent manner.

The second source of her rage was her shame. She felt shame that her parents had behaved in such unacceptable ways; that her father, had abandoned her mother; and that she had trusted her father, who had betrayed her trust. When her current destructive and humiliating actions were about to be revealed, and she feared she would be found unworthy and inadequate, she became enraged. In these circumstances, her rage had a manipulative quality that prevented her partner from pursuing a course that would reveal her failings and expose her weaknesses. In this manner, when Brenda punched Tony, or sexually humiliated him, or when she made destructive, anonymous phone calls, she was reacting to her fear of being abandoned.

Brenda spoke about her sexuality with bravado. She was proud of the fact that she'd had many lovers and that she'd often initiated the sexuality in a relationship. Being sexual made her feel powerful and gave her another way to subjugate her partner. Her heightened sexuality also represented her intense need to feel connected in order to feel safe. Yet by making her sexual needs the focus of the relationship, she unintentionally gave Tony power. He knew that if he withdrew from her sexually, she would do whatever was necessary to regain that intense connection.

■ Victor

Forty-year-old Victor was the CEO of a major manufacturing company. He attended couples therapy with his wife of fourteen years, thirty-six-year-old Jenny, immediately after their oldest son was admitted to a residential treatment center. The treatment center required parents to participate in couples therapy, which this couple especially needed, given their long history of volatility and physical fighting.

Although Victor and Jenny both agreed that their fighting needed to stop, at the initial consultation, they each blamed the other. Jenny believed her angry reactions were caused by Victor's "torturing" her with his controlling and unreasonable expectations. Victor believed his angry responses were caused by Jenny's inability to be truthful, her disrespectful behavior toward him, and her unwillingness to let him "be in charge."

Victor's History with Jenny

Victor met Jenny at an upscale restaurant, where she worked as a cocktail waitress. At the time, Victor had been engaged to a young attorney, whose family, like Victor's, had high social status. Under emotional and financial pressure from his family, Victor had dated the attorney and eventually, albeit unenthusiastically, had asked her to marry him. He recalled thinking that, in contrast to his fiancée, Jenny was sexy and interesting, and that she valued Victor's advice and help.

He had loved how Jenny asked for his guidance. He'd helped her decide what kind of car to buy, and when the car became available, he'd loaned her the money to buy it. When Jenny showed Victor a bruise she'd received from a fight with her abusive boyfriend, Victor had "a visceral reaction" and demanded the boyfriend's phone number so he could call him and "put things straight." Jenny refused to give him the number, afraid that Victor's contacting her boyfriend would only make things worse. So Victor gave her two thousand dollars, telling her to use the money to keep herself safe and to call him if she ever needed help.

Five days later, Jenny called his cell phone from a convenience store, crying hysterically. Her boyfriend, after discovering Victor's money, had accused her of being a prostitute, taken the money, and tried to rape her until she'd managed to escape. Victor had quickly picked her up from the store and then brought her to a hotel. They'd spent an "amazing night" together, as Jenny told stories about her troubled and abused childhood and relationships. Although the two were in bed together, Jenny was too shaken to have sex, but thanks to Victor's comforting, she was able to fall asleep in his arms. The next morning, he broke off his engagement to the attorney, and one month later, without telling his family, he married Jenny in Las Vegas.

Six years and three healthy sons later, their marriage was suffering from Victor's inability to trust Jenny. Victor had discovered that Jenny had inflated household expenses, and he was furious when Jenny couldn't provide an accounting for the unspent money. He'd conducted lengthy "interrogations" as to Jenny's whereabouts when she was not where she had said she would be. Convinced that Jenny was a pathological liar, and in an effort to gain control over her "wanton spending," Victor had put her on a strict budget, which she resented and found ways to elude.

Jenny admitted that there may have been times when she had "misspoken," but she maintained that she was an honest person and a "great mother." She felt that she couldn't "even buy panty hose without submitting a requisition," and that Victor's reactions and restrictions frightened her and made her feel like a "bad child," a feeling she escaped by "trying to be [her] own person." Being her own person usually meant buying whatever she wanted, but she quickly pointed out that her spending was never at the level of the other wives in their social class.

Their first physical fight occurred when Victor had come home and found a play fort made out of sheets and dining room chairs on their front lawn. He had given Jenny strict instructions that the children were to play in the back of the house, in their very large and well-equipped play area. Victor occasionally brought business associates home, and he thought that toys scattered about looked as though he did not have control of his family.

He had stormed into the house, only to find the boys "running wildly, playing with some nanny" and Jenny relaxing in the bathtub soaking herself with "obscenely expensive" bath salts. Victor had exploded. Yanking her out of the tub, he'd tossed her onto the bed and berated her for being a "lousy mother and a disrespectful wife." Infuriated, Jenny threw a flower vase at him and called him a richer version of all the other "scum" from her past. Victor responded by throwing a perfume bottle at Jenny. They'd stopped this fight only after the nanny, with children in tow, threatened to call 911.

Somehow, matters returned to their version of normal for several months, until one day Victor counted more than forty expensive dresses in Jenny's closet, many with the sales tags still attached. Enraged by this "betrayal," he threw her clothes into the swimming pool. When Jenny saw her clothing adrift, she poured bleach on the soft top of Victor's convertible. Their children interrupted the confrontation by pleading with their parents to stop fighting.

Amazingly, there were times when the couple truly enjoyed each other's company. They both recalled European vacations without the children where they "fell in love again." In college, Victor had studied in France and Italy, and he was fluent in both French and Italian. Jenny, who spoke only English and had never left her home state prior to her marriage, loved these trips. Victor delighted in squiring her from one exciting experience to another, showing her the Vatican and the

Eiffel Tower, and taking her to the best restaurant in Madrid. And, of course, Jenny enjoyed the shopping, which in this venue Victor found pleasurable. At one point in their trip planning, Jenny had suggested they visit London so that she could speak English, but Victor had not been interested. In any case, upon returning home, the good feelings that had developed on these trips quickly evaporated to be replaced by angry, physical conflicts, often witnessed by their oldest son.

Living with Victor and Jenny's violent behavior most likely contributed to their oldest son's mean and disruptive behavior at school, which had led to many complaints and meetings with the school's principal. Victor blamed Jenny for being an absent mother, and Jenny blamed Victor for being "rigid," like his father. Victor objected to any negative remarks about his father, saying that his father was a man with "a great moral structure and values." Victor pointed out that, unlike his father, who had believed in corporal punishment, he'd never hit his children. His father had used corporal punishment, Victor explained, because he came from a "different era" and that "we kids were a handful." Nonetheless, out of concern for their children, the couple curtailed their physical violence, but their home remained filled with their nasty remarks about each other.

Around this time, Jenny refused to be sexual with Victor. Victor retaliated by canceling all of Jenny's credit cards and giving her a cash allowance. Jenny struck back by opening new credit card accounts, and when that avenue was blocked, she had written checks from Victor's private account.

One week before coming to therapy, the couple had reverted to physical violence. In Jenny's continued efforts to evade Victor's attempt to control her spending, she had secretly sold items from their home for cash. One of these items was a small painting that had hung in a rarely used room, which Jenny had surreptitiously sold to buy a diamond necklace. One evening, while Victor was driving the family to a restaurant, he noticed that Jenny was wearing the necklace, and asked where it had come from. Jenny, wanting to show him that he could not control her, admitted to having sold the painting.

Victor had screeched to a stop and, over his sons' pleas, pushed Jenny out of the car. Their oldest son had then jumped out of the car to help his mother, and Victor had driven off. After a taxi returned Jenny and their son home, the boy left their house and broke into a neighbor's house. All charges for the burglary were dropped on the condition that their son enter a residential treatment center.

Victor's Previous Partners

Victor's tendency to be methodical and precise carried over into his thoughts about his past relationships. He unabashedly divided his many previous partners into two major categories: the "acceptables" and the "unacceptables." He'd determined a woman's acceptability rating by imagining how his parents would have reacted to her. Given his parent's dedication to their position in high society, "acceptables" came from well-known families with high social standing.

The "unacceptables" were women with financial problems and an unsuccessful professional life, who came from middle- or lower-class backgrounds. He had explained his preference for the "unacceptables" by directly asking the therapist, "If a woman's professional, emotional, and financial life were in order, why would she need [him]?"

Consequently, his past unacceptable relationships had included a woman who had struggled with substance abuse whose rehabilitation he had financed, a woman who had been harassed by creditors whose debts he'd paid off, and a woman who had assaulted a police officer whose legal fees Victor had covered. In the acceptable category, there was Victor's fiancée prior to his meeting Jenny. Although his fiancée had been an attorney, she'd been plagued by anxiety attacks, which often made it difficult for her to leave her home, placed her job in jeopardy, and limited her ability to socialize.

Victor's Childhood and Early Adulthood

Victor's parents had met at a political function. His mother had come from carefully managed old money, while his father had come from a family that still had "the name" but whose fortune had been mismanaged and basically lost by Victor's paternal grandfather. When his parents first married, his mother's money maintained their elite lifestyle. However, several years into the marriage, his father had created an extremely successful conglomerate, using drive, discipline, the family's name, and his wife's ability to cover the initial capital expenditures.

Victor was the youngest of five children and the only boy. With a master's degree in European literature, his mother's life ambition had been to write the definitive work on nineteenth-century French authors. Although she had always seemed more comfortable researching obscure French writers than being a mother, she continued to get pregnant until she finally delivered the boy her husband desired. It wasn't that his mother had been cold, Victor clarified, it was just that she hadn't been "present." Even when she sat beside Victor, he could tell that her mind was somewhere in nineteenth-century France. Nannies and his four sisters partially made up for his mother's absence, but this caregiving had created its own set of problems.

Victor's father had been very much a "man's man" who'd liked hunting, poker, cigars, Scotch whisky, and football. With a volatile temper and rigid expectations for his family, he had especially disliked the amount of time Victor spent playing with his sisters. Fearing that Victor was becoming "a sissy," he had ordered him to find other activities.

When his father had discovered him playing house, dress-up, or tea party with his sisters, he'd fly into a rage, ripping Victor away from the play and whipping him with a belt to the point where Victor had feared for his life. If his sisters had tried to stop their father, they too were physically punished. Even the nannies had tried to intervene, only to be reprimanded and threatened. On one occasion, much to Victor's surprise and horror, his mother had come downstairs from her study to investigate the commotion. Panicked, she had pulled her husband away from the children, only to be knocked to the floor herself.

Victor's father had considered himself a gentleman, and he was clearly upset by the incident. Victor vividly remembers that his father had gathered the family in his home office and explained the necessity of only one person being in charge in a family; and stating that person should be the man. Otherwise, the chain of command would be disrupted, and unfortunate things, like Victor's mother "falling down," would happen. Believing that Victor's mother was unable to provide the necessary "male influence," his father had declared that he would oversee Victor's development. His first rule was that Victor, who was eight at the time, should play only sports or board games with his sisters. He'd said that if anyone violated that rule, everyone would receive the appropriate punishment.

After that meeting, Victor's sisters had left Victor alone, and his world became filled with academics, Scouts, and sports, accompanied by several tutors and coaches. His father wanted him to be a "super son," and even though Victor did his best to achieve that, he often fell short. Not earning the most merit badges possible, receiving less than a perfect report card, or missing a football pass would evoke his father's fury.

In high school the physical punishment stopped, but his father remained a strict disciplinarian. If Victor complained, made a remark that his father thought was rude, or spent his allowance on candy or something his father deemed frivolous, his father continued to impose harsh restrictions as punishments.

Victor's father was very strict about spending money and doled out only small allowances to his wife and children. Victor's mother wasn't interested in shopping, and she considered her husband's monetary concerns to be a nonissue. For Victor's sisters, however, money was a constant issue and often led to screaming fights and, depending upon the girl's age, a physical swat. By the time Victor was eleven, his sisters had managed to live elsewhere, either by attending boarding school or college in Europe.

Victor had not gone away for school. Through the eighth grade he'd attended a nearby exclusive private school so that his father could keep a careful watch on his development. He attended a high school that had been generously endowed by his mother's family for two generations. Victor's father had hoped the history of endowments would cause the headmaster to be especially attentive to Victor. Entrusting the headmaster with the task of monitoring Victor's behavior, his father increased his business travel.

It was at the start of one of his father's extended business trips when Victor had the first of what would be many fights at school. A classmate had made an ambiguous remark about Victor, which Victor had immediately assumed was an insult. So he challenged the classmate. A teacher broke up the fight, and the headmaster told Victor that he would tell his father about the fight when his father returned. Instead, the headmaster had called Victor's mother, who then made a "private arrangement" with the headmaster to contact her, rather than her husband, regarding any of Victor's infractions.

She told Victor that he was to do his best to avoid such behavior in the future, but most importantly, Victor was never to tell his father about her intervention or there "would be hell to pay" for both of them. Victor had been relieved, but was also shocked and disquieted by his mother's proactive and effective effort in circumventing his father. He'd also felt "strangely guilty" that he and his mother were now conspiring against his father.

The headmaster had kept his agreement, yet he often called Victor to his office when he thought Victor's behavior was excessively aggressive, provocative, or unforgiving. Looking back, Victor believes that the headmaster didn't understand Victor's "high moral standards" and "sense of social responsibility." If Victor saw some injustice occurring between classmates, he physically inserted himself into the situation.

What the headmaster saw as "provocative," that is, Victor's tendency to politely point out his classmates' mistakes, Victor saw as "being helpful." And what the headmaster had thought was "unforgiving," Victor thought was "holding people accountable for their actions and having them suffer the consequences."

As Victor got older, his father treated him more like a buddy than a son. His father took him hunting, fishing, and to ball games, and he shared his life philosophies, as well as his concerns about Victor's mother's "strange" personality. Victor enjoyed his "buddy" relationship with his father and planned on attending a nearby Ivy League college so they could remain close. But several weeks after Victor graduated from high school, his father sat him down with a bottle of Scotch and confessed that he had been having a long-term affair with his masseuse. His father justified his behavior by pointing to his wife's lack of emotionality and warmth, compared to the masseuse, who was warm and vivacious, and now threatened to go to Victor's mother to expose the affair, unless she was given a considerable amount of money.

Victor remembers that conversation as one of the most significant conversations of his life. At the time, he was so hurt and angry that he merely shook his head and left the room, although now he wishes that he had been more supportive. The next day, Victor talked to his mother about going to college in Europe, and three weeks later, he was on a plane to Rome. After Victor graduated from college, he returned to the United States and took on increasing responsibilities for the family's business. Although Victor's work required frequent conversations with his father, the issue of his father's affair was never mentioned again.

Given Victor's prestige, education, and impeccable manners, he was considered a very eligible bachelor and was often seen on the society page with a socialite on his arm. However, off the society pages, he preferred the company of women with backgrounds very different from his own. His parents had been exerting increasing pressure on him to marry, with some vague threat about his inheritance thrown in, and they'd arranged for him to meet the daughter of a friend of theirs. To appease his parents, he'd agreed to meet the daughter, an attorney and socialite who suffered from severe problems with anxiety. Much to his surprise, Victor felt comfortable around this woman and sorry for her problems. To keep the peace and perhaps his inheritance in the family, he'd asked her to marry him. All was going according to plan until Jenny entered his life.

Understanding Victor

Education, special coaches, tutors, vacations, and the other material advantages that wealth provides could not compensate for the feelings of fear, inadequacy, and shame that existed within Victor. As an adult, these feelings influenced his choice of partners, compelling him to find women who needed rescuing. He rescued in a manner that was controlling and abusive, which was reminiscent of his father and typical of a terrorizing/terrified white knight.

Like Father, Like Son

Victor's life was a study in contrasts. His father, whose love and protection he wanted, was a source of fear, which left Victor insecure, helpless, and terrified when he did not live up to his father's expectations. We suspect that Victor's father hid his own feelings of inadequacy and shame beneath his rigid and inflexible standards of behavior for his son. Victor was viewed by his father as an extension of himself; when Victor succeeded, it was as if his father had succeeded, but Victor's failures also belonged to his father. Thus, when Victor failed to achieve his father's ideals, his father punitively imposed his own shame on Victor.

In childhood, Victor had identified with his father and his father's behavior. Fearing that his inadequacies would be exposed, Victor had focused on the inadequacies of his classmates. Now, he treated Jenny in the same way his father had treated him: he behaved in a rigid manner that made her feel insecure or afraid, like a "bad child."

In order to preserve a positive image of his father and remain loyal to him, Victor rationalized his father's abusive behavior by believing that he and his sisters had been "a handful." Victor maintained that his father's actions were based on sound principles, and he interpreted his father's need to control and coerce as acts of love.

After learning about his father's affair, Victor felt confused, hurt, and betrayed. Later in his life, he managed to "forgive" his father by marrying Jenny, who was the psychological equivalent of his father's masseuse mistress. By marrying Jenny rather than an "acceptable" woman, he had condoned his father's behavior.

Victor's Pact with His Mother

Adults who were abused as children often tell us about their anger and disappointment at the nonabusive parent for not protecting them. Victor's mother was rendered ineffectual by her emotional withdrawal and her own fear of her husband. When she had intervened with the headmaster, Victor had felt relieved but disquieted. His subsequent fights at school, that only his mother heard about, may have represented an unconscious communication to his mother that she was wrong and that his father was right—that Victor needed to be controlled and punished. The pact also created a special and secret relationship with his mother that, no doubt, made him feel guilty, as though he were betraying his father.

Picking a Partner

Victor grew up with five women in his family, and his father devalued all of them. His mother's preoccupations and his father's concern that his sisters' company would harm Victor made women appear to be weak and inadequate. But because his father believed that spending time with his sisters could harm Victor, he also conveyed the message that women had dangerous power. The fact that his mother, who seemed so passive and ineffectual, successfully overrode his father's agreement with the headmaster proved that she held more power than either Victor or his father realized. Thus, women were to be both dismissed and feared.

Although his father had encouraged Victor to have a relationship with "an acceptable," in his secret life he had his "unacceptable" masseuse. Victor's confusion was apparent in his choices: he had the "acceptable" socialite on his arm for the charity function photographs, and the "unacceptable" strapped-for-cash woman for his heart and bed. Victor had directly stated that he'd sought a woman with an overt need for him. He did not want a woman who had achieved stature and responsibility in her profession, perhaps fearing that her independence would limit her commitment to him, or that she would be like his mother: always preoccupied and emotionally unavailable.

The socialite attorney's anxiety disorder had made her seem more needy and vulnerable, which gave Victor a greater sense of power, and may have made him willing to propose marriage. But her need of him was not nearly as great as Jenny's need of him, which made Jenny a much more desirable partner.

When Victor saw Jenny's injuries and heard of the abuse she was suffering at the hands of her boyfriend, his "visceral reaction" was most likely due to the triggering of his own memories of being abused by his father. Thus, by choosing and rescuing Jenny, Victor could feel strong and in control, but more importantly, he could also be the rescuer that he had needed so badly in childhood.

Anger and Control

Just as Victor's father had spent a lot of time and energy attempting to control others, so too did Victor try to control those around him. This quest to control represented his identification with his father, as well as his own need to forgive his father. That is, by adopting his father's behavior and morality, Victor had preserved the belief that his father was a loving caregiver and righteous, even when his father's behavior was frightening and hurtful.

It's interesting that Jenny evolved into someone who fought back and challenged Victor's unacceptable behavior, which was something he had never done in his interactions with his father. Thus, in some ways, Jenny expressed all of the unexpressed anger, fear, and shame that Victor had experienced as a child but had been too terrified to act upon.

Both Victor and Jenny cited their European vacations as one of the few times when they always enjoyed each other. On these vacations, Victor was in complete control and Jenny was the inexperienced, helpless, yet very appreciative, companion. Victor knew the languages, the restaurants, the customs, and how to get from one point to another. The roles were clearly delineated, and in those circumstances, where Jenny felt pampered and Victor was in complete control, she happily deferred to him and they got along well.

Terrorizing/Terrified Patterns

Brenda and Victor were two very troubled and frightened people who chronically found partners who needed rescuing. Although their worlds seem very far apart, on closer inspection, they are quite similar, and both are in keeping with the world of a terrorizing/terrified white knight.

Coping with a Terrorizing/Terrified Family

Brenda and Victor lived in fear of their parents' lack of control. At a superficial level, their parents seemed strong, but their parents' loss of control over their own behavior and emotions was a sign of great weakness. Thus, both Victor and Brenda were forced to cope with the fear and shame of their parents' rage.

Brenda and Victor also identified with their disturbed parents, which maintained their loyalty. For Brenda, this identification meant being controlling and manipulative, and lying, cheating, and physically abusing Tony. For Victor, this meant being controlling, rigid, self-righteous, and physically abusing Jenny. And for both of them, it characterized a relationship that was bound to fail.

Picking a Partner

Brenda's choice of Tony as a partner stemmed from her hope to control the relationship and thereby feel more secure. She believed that if she rescued him from his lack of direction, shapeless life, and complete absence of money-management skills, he would be hers forever. She could be close to him because that closeness represented no threat. All that changed when he wanted to pursue a more independent course, which triggered all of Brenda's fears.

Similarly, the chaos in Jenny's life allowed Victor to rescue her. In fact, Jenny sought out Victor's rescuing from her abusive boyfriend, her lack of direction, and her confusion about financial matters. Victor naturally assumed that Jenny's needs would give him the control he needed to create a dedicated and orderly marriage, which would preserve his identification with his father and keep his feelings outside of his own awareness.

Rescuing Behavior and Results

Victor's and Brenda's methods of rescuing were very similar and produced very similar results. Victor rescued Jenny by providing her safety from her abusive relationship and a lifestyle she never could have imagined without him. Believing that he knew best, he tried to control everything and everyone. Once Jenny had demonstrated that she was no longer willing to be under his control, all of his old fears were triggered, and he reverted to his father's abusive behavior. In the end, Victor created the very situation he feared: an untrustworthy wife who shut him out of her life and a son who was developing very serious problems.

In a similar manner, Brenda rescued Tony. She provided him with a home, a stable job, and taught him how to think about money. Tony's wish to pursue a college education could be seen as a healthy outcome of the stability that Brenda had given him, in spite of their explosive fighting. However, once Tony sought some independence, Brenda's fear of abandonment was triggered, and she was no longer able to maintain her own stability. Like Victor, Brenda ended up with the very situation she feared: an unhappy partner on his way out of the relationship.

Trapped by Terror

You may look at Victor's and Brenda's abusive behavior and think that they deserved all of the emotional pain that eventually came into their relationships, but it is important to remember that they were both trapped by their fears and limited emotional resources. Their inner worlds were filled with memories of terrifying events, and they were not exposed to healthy problem solving.

Although their difficult childhoods do not justify their later abusive behavior, we can see how their early experiences caused these two people to develop an inordinate sensitivity to any situation that triggered their frightening memories. Whenever they felt threatened, they protected themselves with the unhealthy coping styles that they had experienced and witnessed when they were children.

Summing Up

The terrorizing/terrified white knight, like all white knights, seeks someone he can rescue. However, his rescuing is extremely controlling and designed to make him feel powerful and secure. He is most likely to come from a background that had considerable amounts of frightening chaos or abusive behavior. He is hypersensitive to anything that triggers his fear and sense of inadequacy. When these feelings are triggered, he is likely to respond with inappropriate controlling behavior that is often emotionally or physically abusive.

You have now met in detail the three subtypes of white knights. The next chapter will give you an understanding of the people who become the white knight's partners.

Thinking About It

- How did your caregivers handle arguments?

- How do you handle arguments with your partner?

- Have you ever hit your partner, thrown objects, or damaged things in anger?

- How important is it for you to be in charge in a relationship?

- What was the most frightening experience in your childhood?

- Do you like who you were as a child, and if not, why not?

8

The Rescued

Rescued partners are as varied as the white knights who rescue them, and like the white knights, they can be grouped according to their common traits and characteristics. We created two primary categories of rescued partners, with subtypes within each category. In many ways, these subtypes correspond to the enduring patterns of behavior and inner experiences that are found in traditionally regarded psychological conditions as described by the American Psychiatric Association (2000). This chapter will review the traits and characteristics of those who are rescued.

The Two Categories of Rescued Partners

The partners of white knights have in common the need or desire to be rescued: to be healed, nurtured, guided, or empowered. Within this commonality, the rescued partners can be separated into two main categories based on their overall personality style. The first category, the *helpless rescued*, are those partners who appear passive, needy, and weak. The second category, the *rapacious rescued*, are covertly predatory and have an aggressive style. While you are reading about the rescued partners, keep in mind that people are complex and only rarely can anyone be considered a pure form of any given type.

The Helpless Rescued

Having adapted to childhood circumstances by developing helpless behavior, this rescued partner wants and needs someone to support, advise, and take care of her. She may even tolerate abuse or sexual exploitation in order to stay connected to her partner. Loss and abandonment are especially threatening for a rescued partner who fears being alone, feels powerless, and requires others to help her make decisions. The helpless rescued includes partners who are depressed, dependent, self-defeating, or anxious worriers.

The Depressed

Contemporary psychologists have found that most depressed individuals can be separated into two main types (Blatt 2004; Blatt and Maroudas 1992). The *socially dependent* type includes those who have a strong emotional dependence on others and are primarily preoccupied with interpersonal relationships and the integrity of those relationships. Because she fears loss or abandonment, this dependent type of depressed person is clingy, and experiences feelings of inadequacy, emptiness, and shame (PDM Task Force 2006). She externalizes, attributing the cause of her feelings to her relationship. A partner who is socially dependent and depressed is compelled to cling to a white knight and seek his reassurance and support.

In contrast, the second type of depressed individual is *self-critical* and attributes an internal cause to his depressed symptoms (Blatt and Maroudas 1992; PDM Task Force 2006). He is likely to blame himself for rejection, abandonment, or difficulties in his relationship with a partner, which in turn affects his self-esteem. He may have perfectionistic tendencies and self-critical feelings that involve guilt, self-doubt about his worth, fear of failure, or an expectation of rejection.

A person with a self-critical type of depression has a tendency to idealize others (PDM Task Force 2006). Consequently, she is likely to idealize a white knight and place an extraordinary value on his positive assessment of her. For example, Ron, the overly empathic white knight discussed in chapter 5, married depressed and self-critical Margot, who thrived on his encouragement and approval.

Indications that you have rescued a helpless/depressed partner typically include some of the following:

- Your partner is unable to recognize that she can affect her situation or mood.

- Your partner believes that his life circumstances preclude him from achieving the same level of happiness and contentment he observes in others.

- Your partner is extremely self-conscious and requires your approval.

- Negativity and pessimism color your parner's perceptions of others and the world.

- Your partner's suffering seems impossible for you to change; however, glimmers of positive feeling and her brief moments of joy give you endless hope.

- You experience your partner's issues as a heaviness within your chest.

The Dependent

A person who has an unhealthy dependency seeks constant reassurance and advice, is preoccupied with anxiety about his performance, and fears criticism and abandonment (Bornstein 1993). Because the goal of the dependent person is to obtain nurturing and support from a relationship, he is often mistakenly judged as passive or compliant. However, many dependent people are very responsive to interpersonal cues, seek help, and can be quite assertive in their search to find someone who will take care of them (Bornstein 1992).

Dependent relationships have been linked to *desperate love*: an anxious attachment characterized by difficulty in being separated from the partner, depression, clinging, rage, or violence (Sperling and Berman 1991). The dependent partner who is separated from her significant other will be driven to immediately seek out someone else to rescue her. It is as though the dependent person's sense of self is defined by belonging to the partner and by deriving self-esteem from the partner's identity. For example, a dependent partner may be attracted to the real or imagined power of a white knight because she wants that power for herself.

Understandably, a white knight can mistake his partner's anxiety about separation for an expression of love or desire, and her need for advice or assistance as a compliment to his superior judgment. An overly empathic white knight who wants to leave a relationship may feel guilty about a desperate reaction on the part of his helpless dependent partner, and rescue her once again—this time from his wish to leave. A tarnished or terrorizing/terrified white knight might feel more secure with a dependent partner, because her neediness reassures him of her devotion and gives him greater control. For example, Brenda, the terrorizing/terrified white knight you met in chapter 7, became involved with Tony, a younger man whose initial dependency motivated him to tolerate her difficult, abusive, and inappropriate behavior.

Indications that you have rescued a helpless/dependent partner typically include some of the following:

- Your partner's behavior is submissive and passive.

- You do all of the caregiving and have all of the power.

- Decisions are often difficult for your partner to make without your input.

- Your partner seems to require your help in order to be successful.

- At times, you may consider your partner's needs annoying.

- You find that your partner always wants to accompany you wherever you go.

The Self-Defeating

The self-defeating partner presents himself as a continuous victim of circumstances. He may express feeling overwhelmed, powerless, or fearful. Feeling guilty or shameful about himself, he fears that others will discover his inadequacies, and may hide behind his own inaction. You may feel compelled to constantly reassure him that he is deserving and that various matters are not his fault. You may also be drawn to offer him solutions, thinking that you can fix his problems. At other times, you find yourself annoyed with him because of the indirect ways he expresses himself when he is angry at you, such as sulking or "forgetting."

A self-defeating person can suffer terribly from her own behavior, while wanting understanding and validation from her partner for all of the injustices that have been done to her. Any hint you may give to her that she is contributing to her own difficulties will result in her feeling angry, rejected, mistreated, or misunderstood. Then she may become panicked that you will leave her, which may evoke your own feelings of guilt.

Someone who is self-defeating is impossible to rescue. Initially, your support or guidance appears to make a difference, which confirms your hope that you have provided what she needed. But when your intermittently sober partner is once again found intoxicated, has again lost her job because she was chronically late, or she has procrastinated to the point of losing an opportunity, you may be the one who then feels inadequate and defeated.

Betsy, the overly empathic white knight described in chapter 5, was involved with Phil, a partner who eventually defeated her. Phil lost his job, for which he blamed others; was unable to manage his own career; and habitually smoked marijuana. He was always available to help Betsy, confounding the situation so that it appeared as though she needed him. Betsy made excuses for Phil's failure by assuming he simply needed assistance to market his product. Eventually, she sought therapy because of her guilt about wanting to leave him and her recognition that she was powerless to change him.

Indications that you have rescued a helpless/self-defeating partner typically include some of the following:

- Your partner is quick to help you with your responsibilities but chronically ignores his own.

- Her complaints about bodily symptoms, social interactions, or the stress she is undergoing seem constant and endless.

- Initially, you feel sympathy and compassion for your partner's difficulties, but eventually you feel angry and helpless.

- Your partner chooses to isolate himself, yet he becomes distressed when he is left out.

- Your partner always has an excuse for his disappointment, lack of forward movement, or failure to follow through.

- You feel guilty about leaving your partner or hurting his feelings by confronting him about his behavior.

- Your partner is unable to express her anger appropriately and directly. Instead, she expresses her anger passively by forgetting, sulking, or making an "innocent" mistake that negatively affects you.

The Anxious Worrier

The anxious worrier agonizes about everything, compelling you to comfort and reassure her. She may be quite successful in her work, although she constantly complains about what she does and has to do, and always doubts that she will successfully complete her tasks. Attending an event causes her concern about how she will appear to others. Having a dinner party becomes a major undertaking. Her constant worry and inability to get a good night's sleep add to her fatigue and irritability. Her white-knight partner is helpful, understanding, seduced by her needs, and always believes he can make everything better.

Healthy people who feel anxious or worried either figure out what they can do to make things better or recognize that they must accept circumstances that are beyond their control. The anxious worrier, however, is convinced that something bad is going to happen, and she can't stop herself from thinking and worrying about the issue or situation. When worry interferes with one's daily routine, having someone near can be comforting. This gives the white knight an opportunity to rescue simply by being nearby or providing reassurance.

Dependency that is based on one partner's anxiety can keep a couple together, even though the dependency itself may be unhealthy. For example, one anxious worrier spent the twenty years following her sister's diagnosis of multiple sclerosis worrying that she would develop the illness. Prior to her sister's diagnosis, she had considered leaving her spouse. However, her constant fear of becoming disabled kept her in the marriage, because she knew that her white-knight husband would take care of her.

Indications that you have rescued a helpless/anxious worrier typically include some of the following:

- Your partner awakens in the middle of the night and needs you to comfort her.

- Your partner's worries or concerns are greatly exaggerated.

- If something does not go your partner's way, such as a job interview, she is devastated rather than able to pursue other options.

- Your partner feels helpless when faced with obstacles.

- Your partner's every worry always seems to lead to another.

- Your partner is often concerned that something is physically wrong with her.

The Rapacious Rescued

Initially, the covertly predatory style of rapacious partners may lead you to believe that you have found paradise in their arms, but sooner or later you feel like a victim. Desperate for nurturing and security, the rapacious partner manipulates the white knight to get what she needs, at times, through being irresistibly seductive. Her needs eventually deplete you so that you feel exhausted, depressed, or confused because whatever you provide her is never enough. The rapacious rescued includes the depleting needy, the exotically unstable, and the rigid perfectionist subtypes.

The Depleting Needy

Many white knights fail to see the manipulative and controlling behavior of their partners until they are well into the relationship. The manipulation and control are not intentionally malicious but are actually adaptive in that they calm your partner's fear of abandonment. At the start of the relationship, her fear leads you to feel powerful and secure. You interpret her controlling style and frequent questions about your whereabouts and behavior as a natural insecurity that comes with love. Her impulsive and self-destructive behavior, such as substance abuse, cutting, and suicidal thoughts or gestures, entices you to feel sorry for her, and you forgive her behavior by using the same reasoning that she may use: she has been hurt, she's a victim of parents who didn't love her or give her what she needed, or her last partner abused her.

Intense moods, expressed as anger, despair, or panic, are common in the depleting needy partner. If you are an overly empathic white knight, you will have difficulty understanding why your partner may scream at you, destroy your property, bite you in anger, denigrate your self-esteem in a malicious way, or express other hostile and destructive behaviors. Still, you will make excuses for her, as she will for herself. As a tarnished or terrorizing/terrified white knight, you may lash out aggressively in retaliation if she triggers your shame and fear of weakness. You may feel terribly guilty, suffocated, or controlled. One white knight complained that her partner's explosive temper and criticisms of their friends had left them socially isolated. When she went out with a friend he would call her throughout the visit and demand that she come home. If she did not curtail her visit, he would call her vile names and throw things at her when she returned. He claimed that he had no control over his explosive behavior, which he blamed on his childhood history of physical abuse and her neglecting him. She felt that he was "sucking the life" out of her, but she was too worried about him to leave.

Indications that you have rescued a rapacious/depleting needy partner typically include some of the following:

- At one moment, your partner may express animosity (devaluation) for someone in her life she has recently admired (idealized). Your partner's perception can reverse itself again over a period of time.

- When a conflict occurs with someone outside of the relationship, your partner threatens to sever his attachment to the other person.

- Your partner reacts with anger or serious upset when she is separated from you.

- If your partner feels abandoned, even if he is unable to say so, he may respond with a suicide attempt or threat.

- Your partner is impulsive and seems to do everything in excess, including spending, eating, sexual behavior, and substance use. The potential negative consequence of such risky behaviors is ignored.

- Your partner's thinking is black-and-white.

- Your partner elicits your sympathy when she shares her history of neglect, abuse, or mistreatment.

- Your relationship with your partner leads you to feel burdened or suffocated.

The Exotically Unstable

She is absolutely engaging, dramatic, exciting, sexually seductive, and creative. But beneath the glamour, you will find unstable emotions and manipulative, attention-seeking behavior. She communicates her outer need to be desired by sexually seducing you, which, in turn, makes you feel very desirable. But all of this sexualized attention disguises her inner sense of powerlessness and self-loathing. By idealizing you, she increases the value of your positive opinion of her. However, negative feedback from you or anyone else exposes her fear of inadequacy, and she reacts angrily, by denigrating or humiliating you.

An exotically unstable partner's exaggerated emotions initially may feel exciting and entertaining, catching you up in a whirlwind of feeling. At the same time, she admires and is comforted by your rationality, which may lead you to believe erroneously that she appreciates your reasoning ability and your capacity to ground her. Eventually, you may be criticized for being "boring" or "controlling."

For example, one white knight was dating a beautiful and adoring exotically unstable partner. He felt distressed and powerless whenever he attended an event with her because of her loud and often inappropriate behavior. In one instance, the white knight left a reception, offended by her seductive dancing with another man. She then went home with her dance partner, spent the night in his bed, and blamed her behavior on having drunk too much because the white knight had abandoned her.

Indications that you have rescued a rapacious/exotically unstable partner typically include some of the following:

- Your partner is highly emotional, dramatic, and constantly seeks attention. After she has your full attention, she tends to seek the attention of anyone else but you.

- Over time, you may become wary of your partner's emotional expression, which seems childish, highly sexualized, or exaggerated.

- You catch your partner in lies that he vehemently denies.

- Your partner seems to sexualize everyone and everything but feels misunderstood if you refer to her behavior as seductive or inappropriate.

- When you help your partner, he views the situation as one in which he is doing you a favor.

- Your partner must be the center of attention and becomes angry when he is not.

- How your partner appears to others is of primary importance to her.

- You hear your partner telling a story that is highly impressionistic and distorts the actual event or reality of the situation.

The Self-Centered

A person whose self-esteem requires continuous validation and affirmation may be perfect for a white knight who always wants to be in the powerful position of dispensing reassurance. Eventually, however, the self-centered partner may behave as though he is entitled to your attention and admiration. You give him comfort, attention, or material gifts, only to find that he envies what belongs to someone else or that he most wants approval from someone (other than you) who won't or can't give it to him. You may end up feeling that you are at fault for not providing what your self-centered partner seems to want. In these situations, it can seem as though you are the inadequate person, instead of your rescued partner.

His vulnerability to being overlooked and his need for recognition cause you to feel less important than people who should not matter to him. For example, a white knight gave an elaborate birthday celebration for her self-centered partner. But rather than express his appreciation for all the effort, expense, and care she had put into organizing the party, her partner focused on the "insulting" fact that two "important" people had not attended.

For the self-centered partner, being the best is important. At some level, he knows that he is not the best, and this knowledge, combined with his envy of others whom he is likely to idealize, means that any reassurance you provide will fall flat. Nevertheless, part of your job as a rescuer is to make sure you bolster his self-esteem. You pour your energy, talent, and skill into his endeavors, hoping to be appreciated for your contribution to his success.

You may stay in a relationship with a self-centered partner because of the "good moments" that are unusually gratifying to your self-esteem. Intermittently, she will idealize and adore you in a manner that is delightfully unreal. Your own "addiction" to her occasional expression of seemingly perfect love will compel you to want more.

As a white knight, you cannot expect reciprocity from a self-centered partner; nor will you heal your own vulnerability by helping him. In fact, as you unintentionally take on your rescued partner's shame, fragility, or negative feelings, you will be left feeling more defeated and vulnerable than you were when you began to rescue him.

Indications that you have rescued a rapacious/self-centered partner typically include some of the following:

- Your partner complains about someone who has offended, upset, slighted, or competed with him, expecting you to express (his own) outrage that he has been wronged, all the while ignoring you and any recognition of your importance in his life.

- Disappointment is shocking and upsetting to your partner and causes her to become depressed or enraged.

- Your friends may view your partner as highly entertaining but very arrogant.

- When you tell your partner about an accomplishment of yours, she will talk about her own.

- Your partner hurts your feelings without any recognition of having done so.

- Your partner has an insatiable need for admiration and becomes angry if you call attention to it.

- Your partner has an uncanny ability to twist facts, distort reality, and revise history.

- Your partner can, at will, empathize with you or withhold empathy.

The Rigid Perfectionist

Perfectionism, rigidity, control, and preoccupation with details may initially appear to be admirable qualities. Yet if these qualities are taken to the extreme, they can significantly interfere with a person's life. You may admire your partner's wish to keep the closet organized, but when she becomes enraged because your shoes have caused hers to move from their designated place, you may become concerned about her rigidity. You understand her moralistic reasoning behind everything she does, perhaps agreeing with her in principle but also to avoid conflict. Soon, you will understand that rescuing her means complying with her agenda.

Sometimes, rigid perfectionists have difficulty making decisions, because they dread the possibility of making the "wrong" choice. In such a situation, you may feel compelled to make the decision for him, but he is so paralyzed by his inability to commit to an option that your voice in the matter might lead him to defend the other choice.

The rigid perfectionist believes an ideal exists that he and his partner can achieve. For example, one tarnished white knight found his partner at the kitchen table in the middle of the night, working and reworking the party invitations she was making. She hadn't liked the invitations available in the store and was now seeking an impossible level of perfection in what she was creating.

149

When her white knight suggested that she stop fussing over insignificant things and come to bed, she became enraged and threw the stapler at him.

Indications that you have rescued a rapacious/rigid perfectionist typically include some of the following:

- Your partner becomes upset if your standards do not match her own.

- Your partner has difficulty moving forward with tasks because they must be done perfectly.

- Your partner is very anxious about how others view him.

- You often regard your partner's standards as unreasonable or unattainable.

- Your partner is a high achiever and expects you to recognize his value.

- Your rescuing behavior may take the form of trying to fill your partner's life with more color, experiences, and generally more happiness.

White Knight or Rescued: Who Is Who?

You may identify with white knight behavior in some of your relationships, but in other relationships you may have found yourself in the role of the rescued. A white knight, like anyone else, may sometimes be in a situation from which he needs rescuing. Similarly, a person who is usually in the position of being the rescued partner may temporarily become the person who is doing the rescuing. Thus, you may wonder whether you are a white knight or the partner who is being rescued.

Perhaps you have had a relationship where you viewed your partner as a white knight, because his power appeared to be greater than your own, and it seemed as though you needed him, until you realized that you had slipped into the role of the rescuer. When you met your partner, you may have been struggling with a trauma or addiction, or simply feeling weak and in need of some kind of support, which he provided. But eventually, you recognized that your partner's self-esteem was vulnerable and required your caregiving.

You may have noticed that some of the personality types and behaviors of the rescued are similar to those of a white knight. Keeping in mind the underlying premise of the white knight syndrome will guide you to determine the difference between the white knight and the rescued: *Repeatedly, and often without awareness, the white knight seeks partners who are needy or vulnerable. The compulsion to rescue is the basic condition for white knighthood.*

Variations of the Rescued

Although there are substantial differences among the various rescued partners, there are conditions that can occur across all of the rescued subtypes. These conditions include abuse and a temporary state of needing to be rescued.

The Abusive and Abused Rescued

Although the potential for violence is possible in many partnerships, we found that a relationship between a terrorizing/terrified white knight and a rescued partner, or a relationship between any white knight and a rapacious rescued partner, increases the likelihood of violence. In our experience, women and men who live with a violent or abusive partner tend to lack healthy self-esteem. Lacking a secure sense of self, they have nothing to keep them from owning the shame, vulnerability, and badness belonging to their abusive partners. Sadly, many partners stay in an abusive relationship and endure the abuse simply for the sake of being connected.

Rescued partners who are abused, and white knights who are abused by the partners they rescue, feel stuck in their relationships for many reasons. Similar to the abused children we discussed in chapter 2, an abused partner is unable to fathom how someone who purports to love her can direct violence, rage, and hatred at her. In order to remain with her partner, she alters her sense of self and reality; she may believe she deserves the abuse, or she may minimize the abuse or excuse the abuser. Regardless of what she tells herself, by remaining in an abusive relationship, she is taking on the abuser's shame and badness.

The hope that a partner will change simply provides a rationalization to stay in a relationship that is hurtful. Staying in an abusive relationship is often motivated by the fear of being alone or feeling unworthy of a healthier, non-abusing partner. A partner who stays or returns to an abusive situation may do so because she blames herself or feels guilty, as well as temporarily powerful, if the perpetrator has expressed remorse or vulnerability. With his multiple apologies and promises to change, the abuser gives the nonabusing partner a tem-

151

porary but false sense of importance, control, and hope. The misguided aspect of hope for all rescuing relationships will be covered in chapter 10.

The dynamics of relationships that involve abuse are complex and beyond the scope of our book. Nevertheless, we are adamant that abuse should never be tolerated. If you are in an abusive relationship, we urge you take action or find help so that you can leave.

The Temporary Rescued

A person may appear to want or need rescuing when a life circumstance or stressor affects her emotional stability. Typical situations in which one might become a temporary rescued person include illness, significant loss, trauma, or employment issues.

When faced with unforeseen difficulties, such as a potentially life-changing situation, people differ in their reactions. Some people may become preoccupied with what they are facing and have an increased need to be dependent on a partner. Others may do whatever they can to avoid facing the difficulty, and will stay away from a helpful relationship because of shame or an effort to disregard their needy feelings (PDM Task Force 2006).

The temporary rescued partner does not perpetually need rescuing. Her personality is not structured around requiring help, although a circumstance of need at a particular time in her life can attract a white knight.

Summing Up

Rescued partners generally present themselves as either helpless or covertly predatory. A rescued partner can seem anxious, depressed, phobic, dependent or self-defeating, but he also can be manipulative and seductive.

After the white knight has been repeatedly defeated, she may be willing to see the extent of her rescued partner's emotional troubles and manipulations. Until then, the white knight is likely to idealize as well as diminish her partner in order to feel powerful and worthy.

In the next chapter we will review two case examples of people who rescue in a healthy and balanced manner.

Thinking About It

- What character traits are common in the partners you choose?

- What vulnerable aspects of yourself are hidden in your relationship with a rescued partner?

- Have you ever been attracted to a potential partner because he had the status, the power, or a quality you wanted for yourself? If so, what kept you from seeking or developing that characteristic for yourself? Would you have been equally attracted to him if he hadn't had that trait?

- Considering your current and previous relationships, when have you felt irritated by a quality that initially attracted you to your partner?

9

The Balanced Rescuer

Unlike the overly empathic, tarnished, or terrifying/terrified white knight, the balanced rescuer has a healthy sense of self. This is not to say that the balanced rescuer never experiences hardship, emotional pain, or times when she feels inadequate. However, her healthy self-esteem allows her to behave proactively and facilitates, when needed, a successful rescue of herself and those around her. She rescues altruistically and within an atmosphere of reciprocity and mutual respect.

Denise and Keith, the two people you will meet in this chapter, are both balanced rescuers. They sought therapy for a better understanding of themselves and help for their emotional distress.

■ Denise

Forty-one-year-old Denise managed a division of a women's clothing line, and was the mother of two nine-year-old twin girls. She was referred for individual psychotherapy following an emergency room visit six weeks earlier and a subsequent appointment with her internist. In both instances she mistakenly believed that she was having a heart attack. After a thorough cardiac workup revealed a healthy heart, her internist asked about her current stressors and suggested that she get help to better manage her anxiety. Although Denise was surprised to learn that her symptoms were anxiety related, she admitted that she was worried about Ryan, her husband of eleven years, and how he was spending his time after having sold his business six months earlier.

Denise's History with Ryan

Denise met Ryan when she found herself sitting next to him at the wedding of a mutual friend. Denise recalls thinking that Ryan was good-looking and kind, and she was thrilled when he asked for her phone number.

On their first date, they discovered that, during the past two years, they had both lost someone important to them. Ryan's brother had died in a rafting accident, and Denise's father had lost his battle with cancer. Denise's mother had died at the age of forty-two, when Denise was sixteen, which only intensified the loss of her father. Nonetheless, Denise had coped quite well, and joined a volunteer group that provided transportation to people who were receiving chemotherapy.

Ryan had become an avid cyclist immediately following his brother's death, which he had found very effective for helping him cope with his grief. Now he just cycled for fun and suggested that Denise should join him for a ride the following week. Denise had never done any serious cycling before, but she was always interested in trying something new, and she discovered this was an activity she thoroughly enjoyed. Denise also liked competing, and when Ryan suggested that he could help her train for an upcoming women's race, she was game. Although she didn't win, with Ryan's help she came home with a prize ribbon in the women's beginner class later that year, which Ryan then framed as a Christmas present for her.

From the start of their relationship and later marriage, the two helped and supported each other. Ryan was successfully developing his own business in the wine industry, but he needed outside funding and none of his potential investors seemed interested. Denise suggested some improvements to his prospectus, but since Ryan did not seem interested in making changes, she backed off. After thinking about it, he acknowledged that he had reacted defensively and then implemented her suggestions, which ultimately gained the interest of investors.

Sometimes they helped each other with more difficult matters. One year into their marriage, Ryan's parents died within five months of each other without leaving a will, which caused conflict between Ryan and his siblings. During this period, Denise had made herself available to talk about what was going on, but she also had respected Ryan's need to be silent. She helped him find an attorney and was present when Ryan and his brother went to their parents' home. Mostly, she recalls just trying to be sensitive to what was going on and, if he snapped at her or was short-tempered, to just let him be.

When Denise turned thirty-three, she gave birth to healthy twin girls. The babies were a handful, and Denise found herself "running on empty." She'd always believed that if she set her mind to something, she could make it happen, but managing two infants seemed to be beyond her otherwise capable reach. Everywhere she looked, she saw mothers successfully managing their babies, which made her feel even more discouraged. Ryan recognized her frustration, and he created a schedule that, with his help, allowed Denise to get more sleep; he also found a support group for mothers of twins that she could attend.

Although Denise and Ryan both took care of the girls, they each had a unique role, which kept the household running smoothly. Denise kept track of the medical bills, the girls' activities, and their social calendar. Ryan kept the household budget, and maintained the cars, and he occasionally rescued Denise when she had reacted too quickly without having thought a problem through. When asked if she and Ryan felt appreciated by the other, Denise seemed puzzled by the question and then said, "I guess so. We both express gratitude, but truthfully, we don't even think about it."

This is not to say that the couple never argued. One source of disagreement was spending money. Both of them had come from modest backgrounds, but Ryan was much more of a bargain hunter than Denise, who admitted that she spent "optimistically," meaning that she always assumed the needed money would eventually appear, especially when it came to the twins.

At the time Denise came for therapy, they were putting together a budget that was to be mutually acceptable. Working on the budget had made Denise realize that her spending for the twins had become excessive, and Ryan had realized that he needed to get beyond buying "only necessities." Denise suggested, and Ryan agreed, that in the future they would shop together for gifts, which would also allow him the enjoyment of buying things for the twins.

In general, Denise believed that her life with Ryan was going smoothly. She and Ryan found ways to work through their differences, although occasionally they argued about petty things. Their disagreements never amounted to much, and if a resolution couldn't be found, they were able to move on or just let the matter go. The twins had grown into generous, thoughtful, and inquisitive girls with a special interest in the vanishing rain forests. With their parents' help, the girls had learned the names, and could identify most of the exotic rain forest animals, and they had started a local children's group that raised money for the protection of endangered habitats.

Six months before the onset of Denise's anxiety episodes, a large company had made Ryan a very lucrative offer for his business, which he'd accepted. The new company had hired Ryan to help with the transition, but now that the transition was over, Ryan was without work. Six weeks before coming for therapy, Denise came home early one afternoon and found Ryan watching television. Without thinking, she'd snapped at him for "just sitting around while [his] brain rots." She had regretted her remark immediately and apologized. Ryan had been hurt, but he was more perplexed than angered by the intensity of her reaction.

Denise knew that she wasn't concerned about money since the buyout had been quite profitable. But something had made her "uneasy" about the situation that had led to her remark. Several hours later, she experienced her first anxiety episode and ended up in the emergency room with chest pain and shortness of breath. Her second anxiety episode occurred three weeks later, when Ryan suggested that he throw a party for her forty-second birthday. Later that day, convinced that she was having a heart attack, she asked Ryan to take her to her internist's office. Denise had not seen the connection between her own cardiac symptoms and the fact that she was approaching the same age her mother had been at the time she had died.

Denise's Previous Partners

Denise never had a specific boyfriend in high school. Instead, she'd socialized with a group of friends and always had a male friend as her date at school functions. As a college freshman and sophomore, she'd dated several men casually. In her junior year, she met her first real romantic interest, a young man majoring in architecture. They had planned to join a humanitarian program that built housing in underdeveloped nations. But as her graduation and departure date approached, her father was diagnosed with cancer, and she was unwilling to leave. Her boyfriend left without her, and although they tried to maintain their connection through phone calls and letters, the relationship ended.

Her second significant relationship prior to Ryan was with a stockbroker "who was always ready to party." The stockbroker was also very disorganized, which led to his bills going unpaid, his house being filthy, and his forgetting of important events because he had neglected to write them down. Eventually, Denise came to consider him irresponsible and immature. Even though he was a lot of fun, she realized that she "didn't want to be his mother," and she ended the relationship.

Denise's Childhood and Early Adulthood

Denise's parents had taken the same bus to work every day, and that had led to a friendship that developed into a marriage. Denise was born two years into the marriage, and her brother was born two years later.

Denise divides her childhood into two phases: before and after the onset of her mother's intractable migraines. During phase one, Denise remembers camping with her family, visiting grandparents who spoiled her, and playing and fighting with her brother. Her mother was a stay-at-home mom who volunteered at the local hospital and insisted that both of her children do volunteer work through their church, such as stuffing care packages or making puppets for needy families and children.

One of the biggest fights Denise remembers having had with her mother occurred when she was ten, and she had completed an especially cute puppet. Denise fell in love with her puppet, and she'd refused to give it away. Her mother told her to think about how hard it must be for children who have so few toys to play with, how she would feel if she were the one child who didn't get a puppet, and the importance of keeping a commitment. Her mother's intervention worked, and Denise gave up the puppet.

The other area of contention concerned chores and the parental limits placed on television and telephone time. When chores went undone or rules weren't followed, her parents' response included discussions of the impact Denise or her brother's unacceptable behavior had on those around them. Once Denise became a parent, her own parents' rules seemed reasonable, and she found herself thinking in many ways like her mother and father as she raised her twins.

Denise's father had been a bank manager who had always made time for his children. He taught them how to ride a bike and play chess, and helped them memorize the presidents of the United States, which they'd proudly recite at will. He'd clearly communicated to his children the idea that they had a good chance for success in whatever they chose to do, if they were willing to put in the effort and challenge themselves.

Phase two began some time around Denise's twelfth birthday, when her mother developed debilitating migraine headaches. At first, the migraines occurred only once a month, and the actual episode would be resolved within a day or two. During those episodes, her mother had retreated to her bed with the curtains drawn and a cold washcloth over her forehead. When the children came home from school, she'd do her best to greet them and be involved in their lives, but often she was in too much pain. Denise and her brother had tried to help, but her mother had made it clear that there was little they could do for her and that she really didn't want to disrupt their lives.

Denise believes that her mother enrolled them in several after-school activities so that their exposure to her pain and subsequent withdrawal would be limited. Denise had balked at these activities, wanting to stay home to help her mother, but her mother had insisted. Unfortunately, the migraines became both more frequent and more intense, requiring the children and their father to take over many of the household chores. Denise recalled that the extra chores didn't bother her nearly as much as the loss of her mother's company and guidance, and though her father had done his best to fill in, Denise had wanted her mother.

After visiting numerous specialists who had been unable to stop the migraines, Denise's father found a doctor who was able to help manage her pain. Unfortunately, the pain management had involved a combination of narcotics, which had often left her mother foggy. There were times when she was able to reduce the medication, be more present, attend her children's school and sporting events, and join them as they made dinner. But over time, those times had become fewer.

More typically, Denise came home to find her mother sitting in front of the television, vacantly watching the home-shopping channel. At other times, when her mother was more alert, she actually bought items from the shopping program for Denise and her brother that they didn't need. Denise remembers her father asking her mother about the items, and her mother telling him that buying these things made her feel as though she were still taking care of her children. Tragically, when Denise was sixteen, her mother, who was forty-two at the time, died unexpectedly of a heart attack.

Denise completed her remaining two years of high school missing her mother terribly. After she graduated, at the insistence of her father and brother, she kept her plans to attend a college several hours away, but she had made a point of returning home frequently. She'd majored in textile design, done well, had friends, and, in her junior year, met her first real boyfriend. Toward the end of her senior year, her father was diagnosed with cancer, and she gave up her plans to leave the country so she could stay closer to him.

For several years following her father's diagnosis, he had responded well to treatment. But two years before Denise met Ryan at the wedding, her father had died. Her brother returned from graduate school, and together with the support of their extended family, they had buried their father.

Understanding Denise

In spite of the loss of her mother at an early age, Denise had created a happy, supportive, and productive marriage. Her emotional difficulties when she was struggling to care for her infant twins and her current anxiety attacks were challenging. But because she had a healthy sense of self, she never blamed Ryan for her distress in any serious or continuing manner. As a balanced rescuer, she was able to be open, look at the painful aspects of her life, and obtain help for her symptoms.

Denise's Healthy Sense of Self

Even though Denise had experienced her mother's migraine-related withdrawal and early death, she'd developed a healthy sense of self. Her parents had told her in many direct and indirect ways that she was valued, strong, and capable. She was given reasonable limits, which established that her parents were present, believed she could act responsibly, and would protect her. When her mother had encouraged her children to participate in volunteer programs, she'd taught them about the importance of altruism and empathy toward others. And when her mother had remained steadfast that Denise needed to donate the puppet, she'd demonstrated the importance of keeping commitments, as well as her belief that Denise could handle disappointment.

Her father had always made it a point to spend time with Denise and her brother. He conveyed the idea that success requires effort, which revealed his belief in their strength and potential, without fostering arrogance or a sense of entitlement. In essence, Denise's parents had communicated their belief that Denise's ideals were attainable.

Denise's Identifications

Denise reported two childhoods, but she could have just as easily reported having had two mothers: the mother before and the mother after the migraine headaches developed. Fortunately, both mothers were kind and caring women who'd enjoyed their children and being a mother. Denise's mother, prior to her illness, was a vibrant, strong, and competent parent who lovingly and skillfully directed her children toward becoming responsible and empathic. This was the mother with whom Denise outwardly and consciously identified when she set out to do volunteer work, was successful in her career and marriage, and parented her own children.

Even when her mother had been suffering from migraines, she did her best to take care of her children. She'd enrolled them in activities that would limit their exposure to her suffering, and she'd purchased items from the home-shopping programs for them. But her illness and subsequent treatment prevented her from being the mother she had been and wanted to be, and had left her mentally absent from her family. Denise had loved and continued to identify with her mother, but her mother's illness had rendered her incompetent during a major milestone in Denise's life: puberty and early adolescence. Her mother's untimely death a few years later was a major loss that removed any last hope that Denise would ever have her competent mother back again.

Denise, like many parents, felt overwhelmed with the task of managing two infants. We suspect that adding to Denise's stress was her longing, perhaps unconsciously, for her mother's presence at yet another significant milestone in Denise's life: motherhood. Also, Denise must have missed sharing the joy of her twins with both of her parents, as well as having become acutely aware of how dependent a child is on a parent and, by extension, how dependent she must have been on her mother. Denise's compulsion to buy things for the twins is reminiscent of her mother's attempt to continue her caregiving by buying unnecessary items from the home-shopping programs, and is another example of Denise's identification with her mother.

Throughout both phases of Denise's childhood, her father had been a strong, stable, and stabilizing presence in her life. Denise's positive identification with her father was apparent in her successful career, her willingness to try new things, and her competitive drive. Interestingly, her helping the twins with their projects about the rain forest contained elements of both parents: her mother's volunteerism and her father's thirst for knowledge and willingness to take on a challenge. Her father also had provided a good model for being a supportive spouse, such as when he found medical care for his wife and did whatever he could to make life easier for her.

Denise's Current Symptoms

Denise's anxiety that had manifested as cardiac symptoms can best be understood as an *anniversary reaction* to her mother's death. An anniversary reaction is generally considered to be a reexperiencing of the emotions from a past traumatic event during the present time, when the present time coincides with the date of the original trauma or has elements that are reminiscent of the time of the original trauma. Recently, anniversary reactions have received more attention in the press as more people report being upset or tense on the yearly anniversary of national disasters, such as the attack on the World Trade Center or Hurricane Katrina. Approaching the age her mother had been at the time of her death triggered Denise's sadness, grief, and the sense of abandonment she'd experienced when her mother had died. It also had made her aware of how much she still missed both of her parents.

You may be wondering why Denise's anniversary reaction took the form of anxiety that made her fear she was having a heart attack. It is likely that several factors contributed to this specific presentation. One of these was Denise's identification with her mother. Identifications with your parents serve several psychological functions, and as discussed above, Denise's identifications with both of her parents served her in some very positive ways.

Identifying with her mother served to keep her mother present, and helped Denise handle the loneliness and fear resulting from her mother's absence. However, this positive identification also contributed to Denise's current symptoms. Now, as Denise was about to turn forty-two, her identification with her mother led Denise to fear that she would suffer the same fate as her mother, and die of a heart attack.

Her sense of guilt may have also contributed to Denise's developing this particular type of anniversary reaction. Denise's parents had done all they could to keep Denise from feeling responsible for her mother's illness. Nonetheless, Denise recalls wanting to do more for her mother, and most likely she carries some guilt that she'd failed her mother.

An additional contribution to Denise's reaction was discovering Ryan blankly watching daytime television. Because Ryan's behavior was similar to her mother's behavior on pain medication, it triggered memories of her mother's illness and absence, thereby exacerbating Denise's anniversary reaction.

■ Keith

Fifty-eight-year-old Keith came for couples therapy with Carol, his wife of thirty-five years. Although he initially joked that he needed therapy to improve his golf game, he quickly clarified that for the past several months, he had been "in a slump." He was having trouble concentrating and falling asleep, and had gained eight pounds. These symptoms did interfere with Keith's golf game, but the couple's real concern was their oldest son, Derek, and his fiancée.

Carol, Keith's wife, had not wanted to come for therapy, believing that they could find a solution themselves. But when Keith insisted and stressed the fact that he was having problems with the situation, she'd agreed. Now, however, she was very happy to have the appointment and grateful that Keith had been persistent.

Keith's History with Carol

Keith and Carol had met in a college history class when they were both twenty-two. The professor had been a difficult man, given to humiliating his students. Whenever he called on Carol, however, she'd maintained her composure and won her classmates' admiration. One day after Carol had been especially articulate, Keith had invited her to coffee. As they got to know each other, Carol impressed Keith as a very competent person, which she said was a "leftover from having been raised by unsupportive relatives."

They were both working to pay for college, which made studying and pursuing their mutual passion for backpacking difficult. After dating for three months, they found a few days to go backpacking together. Keith was impressed when Carol insisted on literally carrying her own weight. However, Carol's independence became an issue on their second trip, when she hurt her ankle and was reluctant to let Keith carry her pack. Keith convinced her by saying that they were a "team" and she was hurting him by not letting him help her. He also showed her how to load and carry her pack so as to avoid injury in the future.

One year later they married, and Carol dropped out of school so that Keith could be a full-time student. Although Keith had worried that Carol might come to resent this arrangement, she'd remained very supportive. Three years later, with his degree in hand, he was hired as a city engineer, and he urged Carol to complete her degree, but she had wanted to start their family. Again, Keith worried that Carol ultimately would feel resentful, but Carol had been insistent, and as Keith put it, "Carol can be pigheaded." About a year later, Carol gave birth to Derek, who was a healthy but difficult infant and toddler.

When Derek was eighteen months old, Keith received a disturbing phone call from his stepmother that his father had died in a homeless shelter several weeks earlier, and she wanted reimbursement for the debts he had accumulated. His stepmother's demands required a significant amount of Keith's time and were emotionally draining. Also, Keith was under a lot of pressure at work as he sought to set himself up for a promotion, and he often worked late into the night.

Eventually, Carol told him that although she could handle his absence, Derek couldn't, and that being a father was about more than "bringing home a paycheck." Keith realized that in his quest to be responsible and different from his father, he had gone too far, so he immediately altered his mindset and schedule.

Their second child, a daughter, was born three years after Derek, around the same time that Keith's grandmother had required substantial nursing care. His grandmother, mother, and stepfather lived two hours away, and Keith had driven back and forth to help out during the four-month period before his grandmother died. Having learned from his mistakes when he was working for his promotion, Keith made a conscious effort not to abandon Carol and his children. He took time off from work to help his parents, instead of using his weekend family time. At other times, the entire family made the trip, and sometimes Keith and Derek made the trip alone so they could spend time together and relieve Carol. Keith made the trip fun for Derek, who enjoyed being alone with Keith and visiting with Keith's mother and stepfather.

By the time his youngest son was born two years later, Keith had been promoted and was making a comfortable salary. Even though they could have afforded child care, Carol believed that taking care of the children was her job, and that they should save their money for the children's college education and their own retirement. She also believed that with Derek in lower school, she could easily manage the younger two, who were temperamentally easier.

But Derek had required a lot of time. The school had informed them that Derek was having trouble with concentrating and focusing. At the same time, he was a sweet-natured boy who was starting to make self-denigrating remarks because of all the behavioral corrections he received and his poor academic performance. Keith and Carol had spent a lot of time talking about Derek, and Keith had seen how Carol's insistence on handling problems herself was getting in the way of their finding a solution.

Keith had convinced her to go with him to consult a child therapist, even though he was worried the therapist might suggest that it had been his own earlier absence that had caused Derek's behavior. However, the therapist had been very supportive, and with her guidance, Keith got Derek involved in basketball, where Derek's lanky build and high energy made it easy for him to excel at the sport. Meanwhile, Carol began working with Derek to keep him focused on his schoolwork. Derek's academic performance improved, his friendships with his teammates helped his self-confidence, and he rarely made negative comments about himself.

When their youngest child started kindergarten, Carol busied herself with PTA and church activities, but she seemed unhappy and bored. Again, Keith suggested she should return to college part-time to complete her degree and earn a teaching credential, but she refused, saying the children needed her. Keith had "insisted" that she try at least one education course, and he told her that he would take over as much of the child care as he could. Three years later, Carol had completed her credential and was hired by the local school district. To celebrate her achievement, Keith took the whole family to Hawaii.

Over the next decade the couple had continued to work well together. Accommodating to Carol's teaching responsibilities, Keith had changed his work schedule, did the grocery shopping, took over the bill paying, and hired a cleaning service. He and Carol had put together a list of household responsibilities for the children. When Keith's mother was hospitalized after a severe stroke from which she never recovered, they'd rearranged their busy schedules so he could spend time with his mother before she died, and help Keith's stepfather move into a more supportive environment.

Thanks to Carol and Keith's careful budgeting, a little over two years ago, with their children educated and doing well, Keith retired. Carol continued working while Keith happily took on the role of househusband and looked forward to spending more time with his stepfather. A few months into Keith's retirement, his stepfather died, and for a while Keith lost his direction. Then he became involved with a men's club that provided transportation to elderly people, which he found very rewarding. He also took up golf and planned a trip to Italy.

Recently, a cloud has descended on the family in the form of Derek's fiancée. After graduating from college, Derek had been hired as a salesman for a sporting-equipment manufacturer. His naturally outgoing manner was perfect for the customers, and he became one of the company's top salesmen. Following Keith and Carol's example, Derek had put most of his substantial earnings into an investment account. But because of his relationship with his fiancée, his savings were now depleted, and the two were continuing to spend at an alarming rate.

Carol and Keith were worried that Derek was being "taken for a ride" by this "beautiful but spoiled" young woman. Although Carol was reluctant, Keith felt it was their duty to share their concerns with Derek. Derek listened politely but stated that he had the situation under control. He appreciated their concern, but he was not open to any criticism of his fiancée.

Two weeks later, at the family's Thanksgiving dinner, Derek's fiancée behaved in a cold and withdrawn manner, and when she did speak, it was with a hostile edge. When Derek's sister complimented her dress, she pointedly looked at Carol and said, "Don't worry, it was on sale." When Derek talked about their upcoming trip to Mexico, his fiancée added, "With frequent-flier miles." After everyone had left, Carol began crying, afraid that Derek's fiancée didn't like her and that she "would never see [her] grandchildren."

In the following weeks, Carol showed no interest in anything other than teaching, grading papers, and sleeping. This was so unlike her that Keith made several calls to Derek. Derek minimized his fiancée's behavior and stated that Carol was "overreacting." He did say that since they wouldn't be starting a family anytime soon, there was time to work things out. This did little to reassure Carol, but over time she returned to her old self, having made the conscious decision to stay positive.

Now, several months later, Keith was "obsessed" with the situation, lying awake at night, mulling over his relationship with Derek. Keith was worried that he had made a terrible mistake by talking to Derek and that he was responsible for disrupting his family's happiness. He hoped that therapy could help him "get back in the game" and find a way to establish a good relationship with Derek and his fiancée.

Keith's Previous Partners

Keith's girlfriend in high school had been a smart, well-liked, and sensible young woman who had received a full scholarship to a college across the country. In contrast, Keith described his girlfriends after high school as "high-maintenance, lacking common sense, and able to get you in trouble real fast." Before meeting Carol, he had returned to dating women who had a sensibility more in keeping with his values.

Keith's Childhood and Early Adulthood

Keith's parents had married after dating for six months, when his mother became pregnant with Keith. Because his parents had little money, they'd moved in with Keith's maternal grandparents. His mother was nineteen at the time and working to earn her tuition for a nursing program. His father was twenty-two and trying to earn a living as a fine arts photographer, with no success. Keith describes his father as "a dreamer" who resentfully took small studio and event photography jobs to provide some income. Most of the time, his father had sequestered himself in the garage darkroom developing his fine art photography and doing little to help around the house. His father's lack of financial responsibility had forced his mother to return to work after Keith's birth, leaving Keith in the care of his grandparents. When Keith was four years old, his parents' resentment of each other became mutually intolerable, and they divorced.

Keith has vague memories of his father moving out, but he does remember his father taking him out to dinner and to a playground. Most of Keith's early memories involve his grandfather, who was Keith's "buddy." His grandfather taught him how to fish, ride a bike, and throw a baseball. He'd also brought Keith along on his volunteer deliveries of meals to people with limited mobility, who "always needed to talk." When Keith became bored with the delay, his grandfather would remind him that listening was "an easy gift to give."

When Keith and his grandfather weren't playing or doing their deliveries, they'd visited his grandfather's automobile repair shop. Keith's grandfather was semiretired and had turned over the management of his shop to a young mechanic but still looked in on things. Keith cleaned tools and did simple tasks, which had earned him praise from the manager. Keith loved spending time with the repair shop's manager, as did Keith's mother, who married him when Keith was six. As much as Keith liked his new stepfather, he feared moving out of his grandparents' home. Fortunately, his parents found a house four blocks away, permitting everyone to visit easily and frequently.

Keith's stepfather had been a sports fanatic who often used sports analogies to make a point. Keith remembers not wanting to do his homework because he had misunderstood a previous assignment and had received a poor grade. When his stepfather saw him throw his homework into the trash, he had Keith retrieve the paper and told him, "It's not the fumble but the recovery, and you're not a quitter." This metaphor is something Keith still uses to remind himself to forgive his own or another's errors and to focus on a solution.

Keith remembers his mother and stepfather as being very caring and competent. His stepfather could fix anything and had always been willing to help around the house. When Keith was eight, his stepfather took over making dinner with Keith as his helper so that his mother could pursue her nursing degree. His mother had been a "very industrious woman and reasonably fearless."

When his mother had not been taking care of Keith or studying, she'd made quilts. Every year she'd entered a new quilt in the county fair competition, and on two occasions she'd won a second-place ribbon. When Keith asked her why she kept entering her quilts when she never won first place, she answered, "What have I got to lose?" When Keith was ten, she had insisted that he enter his drawing of a car into the children's art competition, even though Keith had not thought the drawing was good enough. Keith didn't win, but his family went to the children's gallery where it was hung, and took a photograph of his picture. His mother had also been a believer in rules and could occasionally be heard arguing with his grandmother to stop giving Keith so many treats or comic books. The arguments had never amounted to much, and they'd never changed his grandmother's behavior.

In contrast, Keith remembers his biological father as "an irresponsible guy who could never get it together." Frequently, on their dinners out, his father had not had enough money to cover the bill, so Keith had to pay with the "emergency" money his stepfather had always given him whenever he went out with his father. Keith remembers allowing his friends to think that his stepfather was his biological father, and then feeling guilty about the deception.

When Keith turned ten, his father married a woman who "drank too much and convinced [Keith's] father to drink with her." Luckily, she had a steady job at a photography lab, and initially, at least, she had not minded carrying the bulk of the financial responsibilities.

Shortly after Keith's fourteenth birthday, his grandfather had died. His grandmother was so distraught that Keith's mother had to spend time with her to help her. His stepfather, having lost his mentor and father surrogate, became preoccupied.

Keith and his grandfather had discovered that they both enjoyed building model classic cars, and at the time of his grandfather's death, they were working on a very expensive and difficult model. After the funeral, Keith had immersed himself in completing the project, neglecting his studies, sports practice, and household chores. After a week or two of this, Keith's stepfather, without saying a word, sat down beside him and began helping Keith with the model. The next day, his stepfather helped again, but this time he talked about what Keith's grandfather had meant to him. Keith eventually joined the conversation, and he ended up sobbing in his stepfather's arms. The next day, Keith had returned to his studies.

Thanks to his stepfather, Keith "kept [his] eye on the ball," and had a happy and successful time in high school. However, he had remained worried about his father. His stepmother, frustrated with his father's lack of income, had gotten his father a job in the photo lab where she worked. Keith had hoped his father's willingness to work full-time indicated a positive change. Instead, his father had complained that by working in the lab, he was "sacrificing" his dream, which he had used to justify his increased drinking and smoking.

At the same time, his father had wanted to visit with Keith more often. Keith felt obliged to visit, but he'd hated listening to his father describe his mother or stepmother as having "stifled" him, and his far-fetched yet ever-present plans for achieving celebrity status as a photographer. In Keith's senior year, his father had left town to hitchhike across the country taking photographs. Keith never heard from him again.

Shortly after his father left, Keith's high-school girlfriend, a smart, stable, pretty, and well-liked girl, left to attend a distant college. Keith took classes at the local college when his work schedule permitted, and he began dating a series of "troubled party girls," who were very different from his high-school girlfriend. Keith got caught up in their world, and his grades and job performance had suffered as a result. Things came to a head when the girl he was dating wanted an engagement ring, and Keith, having already spent all his money on keeping her happy, asked his stepfather for a loan.

Keith's stepfather had never been critical of Keith's father. This time, however, he shared his observation that after his father's departure, Keith had begun to behave irresponsibly and that he was dating irresponsible women. However, what Keith remembers most was his stepfather's statement, "You can be a different kind of player than your dad." As a result, Keith ended the relationship with the girl who wanted a ring, and he felt better immediately. To this day, Keith believes his stepfather's frank discussion saved him from a very unhappy life. Keith returned to dating young women who were "kind, smart, and competent." When he saw Carol in his history class, he had known she "was the one."

Understanding Keith

Even though Keith was born into a difficult situation, he grew up to be a balanced rescuer. He and Carol successfully raised and educated three children and maintained a loving, supportive, and respectful attitude toward each other throughout their thirty-five-year marriage. Nonetheless, Keith's current symptoms were interfering with his enjoyment of his retirement. His healthy sense of self, a defining characteristic of the balanced rescuer, permitted him to confront his problems, have potential weaknesses exposed, and find the help he needed to move forward.

Keith's Healthy Sense of Self

Keith was born to a very young mother and a father who was too self-involved to be a good caregiver. Fortunately, his mother and stepfather were responsible and caring, and he had loving and available grandparents to help him develop a healthy sense of self. When his grandfather taught him how to fish, ride a bike, or even to clean tools, he conveyed the idea that Keith was capable. His grandfather's emphasis on the importance of helping others had given Keith a sense of responsibility beyond his own needs, and had communicated the belief that Keith could handle delaying his own pleasures to help someone else.

His mother's drive and the hard work that had led to her nursing degree had modeled that goals can be attained. When she continued to enter the quilting contests and had insisted that Keith enter the drawing contest, she had shown him that true success was about trying your best, not whether you win. She had let Keith know that she believed he was strong enough both to follow rules and to handle disappointment.

His stepfather had demonstrated his belief in Keith's strengths. His emphasis on "the recovery" as opposed to "the fumble" had made mistakes an unwanted but inevitable part of life, and the concept of reparation a part of Keith's value system. After Keith's grandfather died, his stepfather had sat with him and, by example, had enabled Keith to feel safe about being vulnerable. All this positive input from his grandparents, mother, and stepfather contributed to Keith's developing a sense of self, which included the beliefs that he was lovable, capable, responsible, and strong enough to take risks.

Keith's Identifications

In spite of the hardship in Keith's early life, he had formed healthy identifications that created stability in his personality. He'd identified with his mother and her ability to achieve goals, take risks, and move on after making mistakes, such as her first marriage. Keith's getting Derek involved with basketball was reminiscent of how his grandfather had gotten him involved in sports, and paralleled his stepfather's love of sports. His identification with his grandfather was also apparent when Keith's stepfather died, and Keith found comfort in working with a volunteer group similar to his grandfather's volunteer work during Keith's childhood. Identifying with his stepfather, Keith had repeated and then created his own sports metaphors for life lessons. He'd also identified with his stepfather's strong work ethic and natural inclination to work as "a team" with his wife.

Very consciously, Keith had identified with his healthy stepfather and disidentified with his ineffectual biological father. Thus, Keith's emphasis on being responsible and making his family's happiness his first priority also can be understood as an attempt to be different from his father. However, as you have seen in our other cases, whom you identify with and the ways in which you identify are often beyond your control.

The pull to identify with a biological parent is strong, and your conscious choice to be different from your parent can often create conflict and cause you to feel guilty. As a child, when Keith had tried to pass his stepfather off as his biological father, he had felt guilty, because in spite of his father's incompetence, he had loved him and was drawn to be loyal to him. His unconscious identification with his father was most apparent when his father had left him to hitchhike across country.

With his father's departure, Keith had realized that his father would never assume a responsible and loving position in his life. At that point, Keith began ignoring his studies and his work. This behavior unconciously maintained his loyalty to his father by making his father right; that is, by behaving irresponsibly in his own life, Keith condoned his father's irresponsible behavior. Additionally, Keith's temporary but overstimulating and self-destructive focus on partying and "party girls" can be understood as his attempt to mask his feelings about being abandoned.

Keith's Current Symptoms

Keith was suffering from a depression that had been triggered by his son's withdrawal and Carol's unhappiness. Such a family situation would be of concern to many parents, but Keith's symptoms were taking a significant and continuing toll on his life. While it is still quite early in Keith's therapy to form any definitive assessment, we suspect that part of the intensity of his reaction stems from his overidentification with his son, his fear that his son was making a poor and potentially dangerous choice in partners, and his sorrow that he had failed his son as a parent.

Keith's well-intended wish to be a good and responsible caregiver, as both his stepfather and grandfather had been, and to be different from his father, had led him to focus so much on his work that he had inadvertently briefly abandoned Derek. Once Carol had pointed this out, he quickly changed his behavior, but he had felt so guilty that he blamed himself for Derek's various troubles. More recently, when Keith saw Derek making a potentially unhealthy relationship choice, he was reminded of his own period of irresponsible behavior and of how his stepfather had saved him. This memory compelled him to intervene and try to save Derek the way his stepfather had saved him.

But Derek's response had been different from Keith's response, and the difference had caused Keith to doubt himself and to fear that he had failed as a parent, as his father had failed him. This sense of failure, in addition to his feeling responsible for Carol's worry and unhappiness, had led him to question his competence and had given rise to his symptoms of depression.

Balanced Rescuer Patterns

Denise had lived through the loss of her mother at an early age. Keith had to cope with a father who had abandoned him emotionally and physically. Yet both Denise and Keith managed to create loving and healthy marriages. Although painful experiences from their past stayed with them and, at times, influenced their adult lives, their relationships with their partners remained solid. They were able to help their partners and be helped in a balanced and empathic manner. Thus, being a balanced rescuer does not mean that you, your childhood, and your partnership will always be perfect. Rather, it means that you pick a partner who can participate in a caring and reciprocal relationship, that you have the strength to look at yourself realistically, and that whatever rescuing you do is altruistically motivated.

Picking a Partner

Both Denise and Keith chose partners who were strong, confident, and generous. Denise had ended the relationship with the stockbroker, saying that she "didn't want to be his mother," when she had seen his inability to manage his life. She could have fallen into the white knight trap of finding someone in need of rescuing as a way of compensating for being unable to help her mother. But her mother had gone out of her way to free Denise and her brother from any sense of responsibility for her illness, which later had freed Denise from feeling severe guilt or shame.

Additionally, because her parents were both strong role models earlier in her life and had given her a good base on which to develop self-confidence, she had not required a needy partner to make her feel strong and competent; she already knew she was. In Ryan, she found an equal: another strong and competent individual with whom she could have a loving and productive marriage.

Keith's brief period of dating and rescuing needy women had been, symbolically, an effort to hold onto his father. The self-destructive quality of his behavior during that time might also have reflected his guilt for not rescuing his father, a pattern often seen in white knights. However, it is important to see this behavior as a response to his father's departure, rather than as a lifelong pattern. In fact, we suspect that Keith was aware that his behavior was unhealthy and that he was actually seeking his stepfather's rescue when he asked for a loan for an engagement ring. By providing guidance, his stepfather did rescue Keith, thus freeing Keith to return to his previous responsible and competent approach to life, and to find and be able to choose Carol.

The Capacity for Self-Reflection

At the time she came for therapy, Denise had not seen the connection between her anxiety attacks, her own age, and her mother's age at the time of her mother's death, yet Denise had demonstrated a capacity for self-reflection. In her marriage, she'd been able to admit that her spending was a problem and to find ways to work it out with Ryan. Rather than simply blame her inappropriate remark about "sitting around while [your] brain rots" on Ryan, she'd acknowledged that her behavior was uncalled for, and not based on reality. She came to therapy open to looking at her own history, behavior, and conflicts, which would eventually provide her with a better understanding of herself and her symptoms.

Keith was able to acknowledge problems and look within himself for their source. When, early in their marriage, Carol had pointed out how he was neglecting Derek, he had been able to see the parallel between his own and his father's behavior. Although he had not used his childhood as an excuse for inadvertently neglecting his family, it had been an impressive insight that had clarified his motivation and helped him to change his ways without ever blaming Carol or making excuses. He was also willing to risk exposure of his potential parenting mistakes by consulting with a child therapist. Whether Keith should have talked to Derek about his fiancée is uncertain. What is certain is that Keith had the strength and ability to allow himself to be vulnerable.

The balanced rescuer's willingness to look at herself involves her willingness to take responsibility for her actions, without needing to deny her errors or to distort reality. This ability comes from her strong and stable sense of self, and allows her to have honest and open interactions with her partners. A balanced rescuer may not like making a mistake, but since she is not shame-prone, she is also not threatened by mistakes. Both Denise and Keith were comfortable admitting their mistakes and moving forward.

Balanced Disagreements

Since a balanced rescuer can honestly look at himself and take responsibility for his actions, he is able to have balanced disagreements. Keith and Denise had disagreed with their partners in respectful and healthy ways that had included an honest appraisal of themselves and their own actions. Unlike many white knight relationships, there was never any emotional, verbal, or physically abusive behavior. For Denise and Keith, a disagreement was simply a disagreement. Because they were confident in themselves and in their partners' love, disagreements stayed focused on the immediate issue and did not deteriorate into broad statements about their partners' thoughts about them, or their dedication to their relationships. This gave all participants the freedom to have frank discussions, come to some resolutions, and go forward.

Balanced Rescuing, Reciprocity, and Results

Even healthy, competent, and independent people have times in their lives when they need help. A healthy relationship involves balance and reciprocity. Neither partner is always the rescuer, and neither partner is always the needy person. Balanced rescuing is altruistic: the motivation is to help and support your partner, rather than to bolster your own self-esteem or to hide your weaknesses. When possible, balanced rescuing facilitates learning and growth so that there will be less need for rescue in the future. Because the balanced rescuer also has healthy empathy, she is able to rescue in a manner that does not diminish her partner's self-esteem.

Denise's marriage is full of examples of reciprocity. Denise spent time helping Ryan reorganize his prospectus for potential investors in his business, and she assisted when his siblings were in conflict about their parents' estate. When Denise was overwhelmed by caring for two infants but unable to see the scale of the task, Ryan had stepped in to help. Although they may have had different tasks to keep their lives flowing smoothly, both of them had actively participated equally in managing their lives. They were able to give and receive help from each other because they were comfortable with who they were, and they did not need to devalue their partners.

Having witnessed his mother and stepfather's positive reciprocal relationship, as well as witnessing the negative repercussions resulting from the lack of reciprocity in his biological father's relationships, reciprocity was important to Keith. In fact, he had worried when he felt things weren't reciprocal, such as when Carol gave up her schooling so that he could complete his degree. Yet Carol's need for independence had often led her to take on more than she could handle and to be reluctant to seek outside help. As an empathic partner, Keith reciprocated by standing firm to give her help, even over her initial objections.

Whether it was carrying her pack when she had hurt her ankle, insisting that she complete her degree, or taking over managing the household, Keith had done all he could to make Carol's life easier. He altruistically helped Carol attain her goals, and he genuinely celebrated her accomplishments, without ever taking credit or feeling threatened that her success would diminish him, make him unnecessary, or threaten the stability of their marriage.

Carol was also a competent and reciprocating partner. She had managed the family's finances well enough so that he was able to retire early, and she had put aside her own goals so as to emotionally and practically support Keith and their family.

Keith's and Denise's balanced rescuing resulted in happy and stable marriages in which the two couples were dedicated to their partners' well-being. The fact that Denise and Keith had problems that had caused them to seek psychotherapy did not mean that their relationships or balanced rescuing had failed. In fact, the stability of their marriages provided them with a solid foundation from which they could explore their symptoms and speed their recovery.

Summing Up

The balanced rescuer has a sense of self that allows her to be confident, supportive, and open to seeing and taking responsibility for her actions. Although she may not have had the perfect childhood, there were enough positive caregivers and experiences in her life to offset the difficulties. Because she feels strong within her self, she looks for a partner who will be an equal, as opposed to someone who is needy and dependent. She helps her partner altruistically, and their relationship is reciprocal: there are times when she is the one being rescued. The balanced rescuer is able to approach disagreements in a productive manner that never involves emotional, verbal, or physical abuse. She has a genuine wish to make her partner's life better, and enjoys and celebrates his success without feeling diminished or fearful.

In our next and final chapter we will direct you toward self-reflection that can start you on your way to finding balance and rescuing yourself from white knighthood.

Thinking About It

- In what ways do you identify with your caregivers' less desirable qualities?

- What relationships do you admire, and why?

- When in your life have you felt the most secure and confident?

- What were some of the most meaningful and positive experiences you remember having as a child?

- How reciprocal is your relationship? What could you do to make it more reciprocal?

10

White Knight
Self-Reflection

We've taken a look at the rescuing relationships you may have with others. Now, let's turn to the relationship you have with yourself. Rescuing yourself involves self-reflecting; that is, observing yourself, thinking about how your behavior in your intimate relationships may represent your own inner conflicts, and giving consideration to what you are actually needing or seeking. In this chapter, we will help you gain perspective about your behavior, and we will present ways for you to develop some important qualities that will help you to rescue yourself. Starting points for self-reflection follow each section in this chapter.

Self-Perspective

Self-perspective involves looking at yourself objectively. As a white knight, the person you rescue is, in part, experienced as an extension of yourself. This leads you to disregard your own inner conflicts, interferes with your ability to accurately assess your own or your partner's behavior, and obscures determining whose needs are really being satisfied. Gaining self-perspective requires that you observe and evaluate who you are in your relationship, and discover what you actually need or seek for yourself.

Driven by her conscience, an overly empathic white knight will anticipate her partner's needs and provide him with nurturing and esteem: what she actually needs for herself yet feels she does not deserve. Betsy, from chapter 5, had a self-centered mother who had been unable to give her the validation she had needed as a child; so Betsy tried to increase Phil's self-esteem in various ways, when it was really Betsy who needed to be validated.

A tarnished white knight rescues his partner to minimize awareness of his own vulnerability, and to hide from himself his feelings of shame and inadequacy that result from failing to live up to his ideals. Brad, from chapter 6, who had failed to live up to his mother's impossible ideals, rescued his wife Patricia from her bulimia, but eventually, he diminished her self-esteem in order to enhance his own. Victor, the terrorizing/terrified white knight from chapter 7, imposed his own intense fear on his wife, Jenny, through rigid control and physically abusive behavior.

Since you cannot rescue yourself through a proxy, you will have to let go of your unhealthy relationship to become aware of what you really need. This involves facing your misguided hope that your rescuing behavior will provide you with what you need, and coping with the aftereffects of another failed relationship. Reclaiming what you may have projected onto your partner and examining the beliefs that led to your rescuing behavior in the first place will help you to separate who you are and what you need from your partner's identity.

Letting Go

You may have ended your rescuing relationship (or several of them) but, in your head and heart, still hear it calling to you. Letting go of a relationship filled with tension and excitement, the kind of drama a white knight tends to experience with a partner, is a difficult endeavor for many reasons. Relinquishing hope and your illusion of control means coming to terms with your failure. But there are still other important factors that cause you to hang on to a rescued partner when the relationship is over.

Misguided Hope

Your hope may have led you to assume that rescuing your partner could help him achieve his expressed goal: be it financial success, sobriety, security, or happiness. Yet despite your efforts, you could not control whether or not he would be inclined to pursue your version of a desirable path. Perhaps your hope was that your partner would become the one you wanted or wished him to be, and he would then need, love, and appreciate you. You may still be clinging to the idea that you could have rescued or changed your partner.

Relinquishing hope is hard to do, because it means that you have failed to get what you expected from your relationship. Rather than accept your failure, you may be inclined to create the illusion that you still have some control over the situation and some influential power (Gal and Lazarus 1975). An overly empathic white knight might blame herself for her partner's inability to give her what she needs, if accepting the blame allows her to stay in the relationship. Tarnished or terrorizing/terrified white knights will attempt to control or manipulate their partners, even in destructive ways, rather than accept defeat.

Your continued efforts to rescue your partner allow you to avoid and deny your own feelings of helplessness, despair, depression, or yearning that are the negative counterparts of hope (Lazarus 1999). The feelings associated with giving up hope are often the very same emotions you sought to avoid in the first place. Once you accept that your rescuing failed to get you what you wanted, you will have an opportunity to look at the feelings that are hidden behind your white knight façade.

Starting Points for Relinquishing Misguided Hope

- Try to understand that your continued hope to rescue or change your partner represents your own need to feel powerful and avoid feelings that you find undesirable. Reflect on the feelings of helplessness, despair, depression, or yearning that you have avoided. Where did they originate? Can you recognize how you may have adapted to your circumstances? How can you change yourself or your attitude now?

- Accept that what you see is what you'll get. Once your relationship becomes firmly established, your partner's personality and the way in which she treats you will most likely be what your future together will look like. Staying with a partner whom you hope will change usually results in disappointment.

- When a relationship fails, allow some time to understand what it was that you had hoped for, and then evaluate whether or not your hopes were realistic given your choice of a partner.

Coping with Aftereffects

Thinking about your failed relationship is similar to replaying scenes from a movie in your mind. Replaying the scenes from the good times in your relationship can lead you to continue grieving or to grieve anew for what you no longer have. It can also lead you to spend time desperately trying to understand what went wrong. You may wonder if your former partner is thinking about you in the ways in which you are thinking about him, or you may just incessantly wonder what he is thinking. Your ruminations about the failed relationship can take on an obsessive quality, as though your thoughts and the feelings that stir within you are beyond your control.

At other times, you may focus on scenes that anger and disturb you, which block the good but painful memories, and provide temporary relief because you are no longer involved. You can remind yourself once again that you rescued a "self-centered creep" or that your partner did not value you. However, thinking about the horrible scenes from your failed relationship may cause strong negative emotions to come forth, impinging on your ability to enjoy life.

Sharing your upsetting memories with a friend can provide a temporary source of comfort. By doing so, you give away your feelings. Your friend becomes a proxy for your anger toward your former partner, and she can then express the ill feelings you have about him. But the relief is short-lived.

Why is it so hard to change your mood and stop thinking about your former partner when a relationship fails? Your unhappy disposition and obsessive thoughts following a failed relationship have a neurochemical basis; that is, levels of dopamine and serotonin in your brain are actually altered in ways that are similar to those of an addict withdrawing from a stimulant (Fisher 2004). Both romantic love and failed relationships can cause intense craving and reality distortion, according to Helen Fisher (2006), who used functional magnetic resonance imaging (fMRI) to study the brains of love-struck and recently rejected people. Failed relationships have also been shown to result in increased brain activity linked to obsessive-compulsive behaviors, anger-management problems, depression, anxiety, and high-risk decision making (Fisher et al. 2002).

Understanding why you continue to ruminate about your partner long after the relationship is over may help you to rescue yourself by imposing damage control so that you won't act out in ways that could hurt yourself. White knight relationships can be highly stimulating emotionally and sexually, and some are intensely dramatic. When the relationship has ended, your brain may seek similar stimulation, and you may crave something to fill the empty space that was occupied by your rescued partner. In your efforts to regain physiological and psychological balance, your search for pleasure and emotional closeness may lead you to engage in risky, promiscuous, or addictive behavior (Goeders 2004). Highly stimulating or intoxicating activities will numb you temporarily but they will not help you to rescue your self.

Letting go requires emotional and cognitive effort on your part to redirect yourself in a healthy way. Engaging in challenging activities that require intense focus and attention—for example, starting a creative endeavor or a new sport; completing unfinished tasks; or seeking career, professional, or volunteer opportunities—will help you feel good about yourself and also help you to direct your feelings in positive ways in the aftermath of your relationship failure. Also, you are more likely to find a healthy relationship when you yourself are healthy. When you do think about your failed relationship, do so in the context of learning from your past behavior, understanding what you really want and need, and figuring out what you can do differently in the future.

Starting Points for Coping with the Aftereffects of a Failed Relationship

- Rather than sit with your strong negative emotions about your failed relationship, think about what you would do differently if you could relive any particular moment.

- What have you learned about yourself from your relationship? What did you want for yourself that you tried to give to your partner?

- What can you accomplish and control that will help to restore your self-esteem?

- When a relationship fails, you may find yourself involved in addictive behavior, such as alcohol or substance abuse, gambling, or risky sexual behavior. You may believe that your behavior helps to numb your pain, but you are actually interfering with healing yourself by substituting another brain-stimulating activity. Seek help from friends, a support group, or a therapist.

Reclaiming Your Projections

Changing yourself and your direction involves building your strengths and correcting your weaknesses. You can start by reclaiming what you have been trying to avoid acknowledging about yourself by stepping back and looking at yourself and your relationship with honest eyes. Our examples of white knights have included those who projected onto partners their own fear of inadequacy or weakness; their own longing for loving support and validation; their own wish for empathic responsiveness; and their own shame, need for perfection, and self-criticism.

Although your partner is a separate person, you may regard her as an extension of yourself. Brad, the tarnished white knight from chapter 6, viewed his wife Patricia, as an extension of himself, so he assumed that any decisions he made that were good for him would automatically be good for her too. If the boundaries between you and your partner are blurred, idealizing your partner's qualities is self-serving.

Projecting a part of yourself onto a partner, that is, ascribing to her your own thoughts, feelings, or needs, has been a way that you've managed your anxiety about your own vulnerabilities. The greater your anxiety, the greater your tendency will be to have another person serve as a proxy to help you cope with your own psychological needs (Basch 1994). Conveniently, your partner may have vulnerabilities similar to your own, making the process of identifying yourself in her easy so that when you rescue her, you vicariously rescue yourself.

Starting Points for Reclaiming Your Projections

- Consider what you project onto your partner. Is your preoccupation with your partner's flaws an avoidance of your anxiety about your own imperfections? What do you consider to be your flaws or the ways in which you devalue yourself?

- Talk to your partner about his needs, desires, and preferences. Accept that what works for you may not necessarily work for him.

- Whether your partner's behavior embarrasses you or leads you to feel more important, your sense of self may hinge upon his identity and behavior. Think about the qualities in your partner that you believe enhance your status or devalue it. Make a conscious effort to recognize your partner as a separate being, one who can be responsible for his own behavior.

- Rather than ignore the feeling that you have failed to live up to your ideals, acknowledge it to yourself, and reflect on the sources of your shame.

Examining Beliefs and Convictions About Yourself

You want to be seen, accepted, and loved as you truly are, which includes your fears and vulnerabilities. The beliefs and convictions you developed from your early experiences with your caregivers play a part in what you later feel you deserve. Those beliefs and convictions also affect your self-esteem, and may interfere with your pursuit of healthy relationships and goals (Weiss 1993). As discussed in previous chapters, you may have grown up believing, for example, that you do not deserve to have your needs met or that being vulnerable is unsafe. How others respond to you leads you to confirm or disconfirm such pathogenic beliefs and convictions. Becoming more aware of your beliefs and convictions, and being mindful of how you may be testing your partner can enable you to correct how you experience yourself.

In varying degrees you may test your partner to assess the validity of your beliefs and convictions. You may treat your partner in a way that is similar to how you were treated by your caregivers, hoping, at some level, that she can demonstrate a healthier response than the one that was available to you in your early experiences.

In chapter 7, for example, Victor behaved aggressively toward his partner Jenny, in a manner that resembled how he had been treated by his father. As a child, Victor had few available responses to his father's abuse. But Jenny was an adult and could stand up for herself, albeit in the unhealthy form of fighting back. If Jenny had walked away from the relationship, rather than fighting back and remaining engaged in the abuse, she would have been a healthy role model for Victor. Self-perspective might have allowed Victor to realize that his treatment of Jenny was no more acceptable than his father's treatment of him had been. Stepping back and looking at his behavior would have provided him with an opportunity to learn from the experience with his wife.

If you're drawn to a partner who repeats the relationship you had with a parent, you may be unconsciously hoping to correct your earlier experience and the beliefs you formed about yourself. But as a white knight, you have likely found a partner who confirms rather than disconfirms your pathogenic beliefs about yourself, and who cannot provide the necessary emotional experiences to correct your own negative self-view. You may blame your partner for his inability to give you what you need, but you also must determine whether you have found a partner whose attitude toward you perpetuates the very convictions you have about yourself that you want to disconfirm.

Social psychologists have investigated the importance of developing a positive self-view and how your self-view affects your choice of a partner. These studies have shown that people tend to seek *self-verifying partners*; that is, they seek a partner who will eventually validate their self-view, either positively or negatively (de la Ronde and Swann 1998).

In your partner, you may find an accomplice who, ultimately, will preserve how you actually perceive yourself, even if that perception is a negative one. Extending the process of self and partner verification to white knight relationships has implications for understanding why rescuing leads to failure. A person with a negative self-view may, without any conscious intent, elicit unfavorable evaluations from a partner, or may assign more negative meaning to the partner's behavior than the partner had intended (Swann 1997). For example, Brenda, the terrorizing/terrified white knight described in chapter 7, was so suspicious and jealous that she behaved in a manner that elicited many negative reactions from others, which only confirmed her own negative self-view.

Even though your conscious desire is to obtain a positive evaluation from your partner, if you have a negative self-view, your desire for self-verification can override your conscious wish for a positive evaluation from her (Swann 1997). Your loyalty to the early relationship patterns that determined your self-view may be a powerful hindrance to your ability as an adult to disconfirm and change beliefs about yourself. Thus, it is important to recognize these patterns in your relationships and to rescue yourself from repeating them.

Self-verification is particularly important to those who strive to maintain their perception of control over their environment (Stets and Burke 2005). A spouse who needs to maintain this perception, such as a terrorizing/terrified white knight, will respond to threats to his self-verification by increasing his control over his partner. When the lack of verification persists or the perception of control is not regained, that spouse may use physical aggression, such as imposing oppressive behavior or restricting another's activity, as the ultimate way to reassert control (Stets and Burke 2005).

In chapter 7, you saw how extremely important it was to Victor to control his family's life. For example, he flew into a rage at his wife when he discovered their children playing on the front lawn instead of in their backyard. For people like Victor to rescue themselves, they must stop their behavior and find help that will enable them to recognize the feelings behind their need to oppressively control another person.

Starting Points for Examining Your Beliefs

- As a result of your childhood, what pathogenic beliefs have you developed about yourself? For example, you may see yourself as undeserving, unable to control yourself in some way, or as having some characteristic or trait that was erroneously assigned to you when you were a child. How have unhealthy beliefs about yourself changed or been confirmed as a result of your intimate relationships?

- Think about how you were treated by your caregivers. Now think about how you treat your partners. What similarities do you see? How do these similarities contribute to conflicts with your partner?

Rescuing Yourself

Rescuing yourself involves building your self-esteem—the emotional and cognitive beliefs about your value—and enhancing your *sense of agency*—that is, the ability to take action, influence your own life, and assume responsibility for your actions. Optimal self-esteem and a strong sense of agency protect you in healthy ways and contribute to your stability as a separate person. This enables you to create a relationship based on mature love rather than one based on a quest to heal or the need to define yourself. Mature love recognizes the reality of your partner; that is, she is a separate individual with her own needs and wishes.

Optimizing Your Self-Esteem

When considered in the context of the self, esteem involves an estimate or a valuation of your own worth. As discussed in chapter 4, your self-esteem results from your assessment of your ability to live up to your conscience, as well as your ability to attain your ideals.

To lack self-esteem may be just as detrimental as esteeming yourself too highly. Overly empathic white knights tend to underestimate themselves with self-doubt or guilt. Tarnished and terrorizing/terrified white knights either falsely inflate their self-esteem by idealizing themselves, or intensely diminish their self-view with feelings of extreme shame or inadequacy.

Self-esteem is an important concept in psychology that, unfortunately, has been trivialized by misconceptions. The notion of promoting self-esteem has become a catchphrase in popular culture, along with the idea that superficial emotional support can augment the self-esteem of others. For example, our child-rearing and educational systems are based on external evaluations of accomplishment and worth. Although children may feel more motivated to learn when they gain the approval of a parent or an admired teacher for performing well, generalized approval that ignores reality may be a deterrent; in fact, it may even promote unhealthy development in children. Providing positive reactions or praise to someone for trivial accomplishments fosters illusion, self-deception, and feelings of fraudulence (McWilliams 1999).

Self-esteem is unhealthy at its extremes. Unjustified and unstable high self-esteem defines narcissism (Bushman and Baumeister 1998). If you have an inflated sense of your own worth or you have a deflated sense of self-worth, you will be highly sensitive to criticism and slights because you are internally vulnerable. Some people with low self-esteem, and those at the other end of the spectrum with high or unrealistic opinions of themselves, are prone to aggressive and controlling behaviors (Bushman and Baumeister 1998).

Optimal self-esteem is a healthy, balanced sense of inner comfort and security that reflects confidence and satisfaction in your sense of self. At an optimal level, self-esteem can be considered as healthy narcissism (McWilliams 1999). Even so, your self-esteem will vary: there may be times when you experience self-doubt, feel less than satisfied about who you are, overvalue yourself, are subject to inner conflict or stress, or feel insecure if challenged. So, your self-esteem does not always have to be positive or stable for it to be optimal; and brief, periodic fluctuations are quite common. Your self-esteem naturally fluctuates as a result of your moods, experiences, and interactions.

In order to regulate your self-esteem, you may depend on external sources in healthy or unhealthy ways. Being close to others, gaining acceptance from those you love, seeking admiration or validation from others, and using controlling behavior or power tactics in your relationships may elevate your self-esteem temporarily. However, an excessive reliance on external sources for self-esteem regulation puts you in a very vulnerable position. It may indicate a need to examine and work on the factors affecting your self-view, either through self-help or by seeking professional assistance. Healthy self-esteem will give you the ability to be authentic, honest, and autonomous, and it will help you to maintain a solid sense of self.

Starting Points for Optimizing Self-Esteem

- Think about the times when you felt good about yourself. What commonalities do you see?

- What external sources do you depend on for your self-esteem? Consider what you get from those sources and find a way to provide it for yourself.

- Think about the last time you suffered a slight to your self-esteem either from an internal or external source. What actions did you take to feel better about yourself? Did these actions work?

- Think about the relationships you had with family members and how they impacted your self-esteem. What could they have done to help you create optimal self-esteem? Now, find a way in which you can do those things for yourself.

Your Sense of Agency

Your ability to take action, be effective, influence your own life, and assume responsibility for your behavior are important elements in what you bring to a relationship. This sense of agency is essential for you to feel in control of your life, believe in your capacity to influence your own thoughts and behavior, and have faith in your ability to handle a wide range of tasks or situations. Having a sense of agency influences your stability as a separate person; it is your capacity to be psychologically stable, yet resilient or flexible, in the face of conflict or change.

As a white knight, there are various ways in which you consciously or unconsciously try to increase your own sense of agency through your relationship. Feeling needed and wanted by a partner can create a sense of power and control, but if the relationship fails, your old feelings of being ineffectual and weak will return. The nurturing, support, and resourcefulness of an overly empathic white knight initially enhance her feelings of agency, but such acts ultimately render her dependent on her partner's response in order to maintain her sense of being an effective person. The tarnished and terrorizing/terrified white knight may control his partner; however, his sense of agency depends on his maintaining that control.

A white knight's efforts to increase her own sense of agency by increasing her partner's dependency on her will ultimately fail. The healthiest people strive to increase their sense of personal power by developing competence and autonomy and by decreasing their dependence on others (van Dijke and Poppe 2006). Increasing your sense of competence and autonomy involves, among other things, recognizing the ways in which you can influence your own life without needing to control your partner, and assuming responsibility for your behavior without needing to blame others. These are qualities found in the balanced rescuer.

Starting Points for Increasing Your Sense of Agency

- Think about an area of your life in which you feel very successful and an area of your life in which you would like to be successful but are not. How can you apply the techniques that helped you to achieve success to the areas where you are not successful?

- Imagine that your partner was less dependent on you. How does this thought make you feel? Although, initially, you may be uneasy with the concept, dependency does not necessarily equate with a strong relationship, and often leads to resentment.

- Who are you dependent on, and what can you do to decrease your dependence on that person but still maintain your relationship?

- Ask yourself if the interactions you have with your partner are designed to bring out her weaknesses, thus hiding your own, or if you can recognize and validate your partner's strength and power without fearing weakness in yourself. Think about simply telling your partner something that validates her strength and power. Does the idea frighten you or make you feel weak? Try it and see what happens.

Influencing Your Own Life

Researchers consistently find that placing a strong importance on *intrinsic aspirations*—goals that directly satisfy basic needs such as personal growth, affiliation, and community involvement—is positively associated with indicators of well-being, including self-esteem and self-actualization, and negatively associated with depression and anxiety (Ryan et al. 1999). On the other hand, placing strong relative importance on *extrinsic aspirations*—goals that indirectly satisfy needs like wealth, fame, and public image—is negatively related to indicators of well-being.

There are many ways in which you can influence and control your own life that will provide you with a sense of agency. These include striving for personal health, creating reasonable and attainable goals for yourself, developing resilience to cope with stressful situations, mastering new tasks or challenges, developing your talents, and striving for mutual respect and cooperation in your interactions with others.

Starting Points for Influencing Your Own Life

- If you were to make a conscious effort to increase your affiliations with others and further your community involvement, where would you begin? What are your special interests? Find a community organization or volunteer group that addresses those interests and become involved.

- Create a list of goals to promote your own personal growth.

- What would make you a better, happier, or healthier individual? Focus on positive qualities you want to adopt as your own. Become inspired by reading biographies and noting the qualities or behaviors you admire in the people being written about. In your daily life, notice admirable qualities in others and seek out mentors who inspire you.

Taking Responsibility

Having a sense of agency is associated with being able to take responsibility for your actions. As a tarnished or terrorizing/terrified white knight, you're often likely to hurt your partner's feelings, and you have a difficult time admitting wrongdoing as well as sincerely expressing remorse. These white knights have told us that to apologize, even when an apology is appropriate, would upset the power relationship, feel as if they were giving in, or make them appear weak in their own or their partners' eyes.

If your shame prevents you from apologizing, when pressed, you're likely to make a statement that has an aspect of an apology but is disingenuous. This pseudoapology can take many forms. It can be a terse, blunt, one-word apology, such as, "Sorry," which implies, "I'm only going through the motions of an apology, but I don't really mean it." It can include a disclaimer that contains an element of blaming the victim; for example, "I'm sorry, *but* when you did...," or "I'm sorry if I hurt your feelings."

Such pseudoapologies can imply that the problem is not due to the guilty party's actions but, rather, that the person owed the apology is too sensitive and has feelings that are too easily hurt. Whatever type of pseudoapology is used, keep in mind that it really reflects the fear that your weakness will be exposed by the admission of guilt, leaving you open to harmful self-judgment or criticism from others.

You may want to reflect on the notion that when you apologize, you are simply saying that you take responsibility for your mistake, agree that it should not have happened, and regret that your mistake adversely affected the other person. One crucial aspect of taking responsibility for your actions can be found in your future behavior. Apologies or expressions of regret about your wrongdoing are likely to have a beneficial effect on your relationship, but they do not necessarily restore or reestablish trust (Exline and Baumeister 2000). Only a significant and positive change in your behavior will do that.

Starting Points for Taking Responsibility

- The next time you have an argument with your partner, try to acknowledge your part in the conflict without pointing out what your partner did. At a later time, you can tell her how her behavior affected you—without making this an excuse for your own actions.

- Apologies, if sincere, are a wonderful way to make the other person feel respected and acknowledged. However, if the apology is really a pseudoapology or isn't followed up with a change in behavior, it becomes meaningless, if not manipulative and insulting. Make sure you can back up your apology with a real behavioral change. If you need help doing this, talk to your partner about it.

- If you tend to take all of the responsibility for the conflicts in your relationship, think about a time when you were unable to stand up for yourself, and then consider what you could have said to protect your own self-interest. What are the fears or beliefs that interfere with your self-protection?

- Recognizing your partner's emotional state can help you to avoid and resolve conflicts, and to take responsibility when conflicts arise. Stepping back and focusing on your partner's feelings or imagining how you would feel in your partner's shoes are ways to increase your empathic response.

Final Reflections

Reflecting on the inner conflicts and needs hidden behind your white knight behavior is an essential step in rescuing yourself from your need to rescue others. Once you can give up your misguided hope and face your feelings of helplessness, despair, depression, or yearning, you can move toward healthier possibilities. Reclaiming what you have attributed to your partner, and examining the beliefs and convictions you developed during your early experiences will help you to recognize the reality of your partner as a separate being from yourself.

Leaving knighthood and becoming a balanced rescuer involves focusing your efforts on developing optimal self-esteem and agency, including your ability to maintain a healthy sense of self, influence your own life, and assume responsibility for your behavior. Letting go of the excitement and drama intrinsic to rescuing relationships is difficult for many reasons. But we hope you will use your determination to redirect yourself toward healthy choices.

Now that we have explored what's behind your knighthood and encouraged your self-reflection, you are ready to begin creating balance in yourself and in your relationship. Along with some starting points, we will leave the rescuing to you. We know you can do it.

References

American Psychiatric Association (APA). 2000. *Diagnostic and Statistical Manual of Mental Disorders*. 4th ed., text revision. Washington, DC: American Psychiatric Association.

Basch, M. F. 1994. The selfobject concept: Clinical implications. *Progress in Self Psychology* 10:1-7.

Batson, C. D. 1991. *The Altruism Question: Toward a Social-Psychological Answer.* Hillsdale, NJ: Lawrence Erlbaum Associates.

Blatt, S. J. 2004. *Experiences of Depression: Theoretical, Clinical, and Research Perspectives.* Washington, DC: American Psychological Association.

Blatt, S. J., and C. Maroudas. 1992. Convergences among psychoanalytic and cognitive behavioral theories of depression. *Psychoanalytic Psychology* 9:157-190.

Bornstein, R. F. 1992. The dependent personality: Developmental, social, and clinical perspectives. *Psychological Bulletin* 112:3-23.

———. 1993. *The Dependent Personality.* New York: The Guilford Press.

Bowlby, J. 1982. *Attachment and Loss, Vol. 1: Attachment.* Rev. ed. New York: Basic Books.

Bushman, B. J., and R. F. Baumeister. 1998. Threatened egotism, narcissism, self-esteem, and direct and displaced aggression: Does self-love or self-hate lead to violence? *Journal of Personality and Social Psychology* 75(1):219-229.

Cialdini, R. B., S. L. Brown, B. P. Lewis, C. Luce, and S. L. Neuberg. 1997. Reinterpreting the empathy-altruism relationship: When one into one equals oneness. *Journal of Personality and Social Psychology* 72:481-494.

Decety, J., and Y. Moriguchi. 2007. The empathic brain and its dysfunction in psychiatric populations: Implications for intervention across different clinical conditions. *Biopsychosocial Medicine* 1:22-52.

de la Ronde, C., and W. B. Swann. 1998. Partner verification: Restoring shattered images of our intimates. *Journal of Personality and Social Psychology* 75:374-382.

Eisenberg, N., P. A. Miller, M. Schaller, R. A. Fabes, J. Fultz, R. Shell, et al. 1989. The role of sympathy and altruistic personality traits in helping: A reexamination. *Journal of Personality* 57(1):41-67.

Ekman, P. 1972. Universal and cultural differences in facial expressions of emotion. In *Nebraska Symposium on Motivation*, 1971, ed. J. Cole, 19:207-283. Lincoln, NE: University of Nebraska Press.

Erikson, E. H. 1956. The problem of ego identity. *Journal of the American Psychoanalytic Association* 4:56-121.

Eslinger, P. J. 1998. Neurological and neuropsychological bases of empathy. *European Neurology* 39:193-199.

Exline, J. J., and R. F. Baumeister. 2000. Expressing forgiveness and repentance: Benefits and barriers. In *Forgiveness: Theory, research, and practice*, ed. M. McCullough, K. I. Pargament, and C. E. Thoresen, 133-155. New York: The Guilford Press.

Fisher, H. E. 2004. *Why We Love: The Nature and Chemistry of Romantic Love.* New York: Henry Holt and Company.

————. 2006. The drive to love: The neural mechanisms for mate choice. In *The new psychology of love*, 2nd ed., ed. R. J. Sternberg and K. Weis. New Haven: Yale University Press.

Fisher, H. E., A. Aron, D. Mashek, G. Strong, H. Li, and L. L. Brown. 2002. Defining the brain systems of lust, romantic attraction, and attachment. *Archives of Sexual Behavior* 31:413–419.

Flores, P. J. 2004. *Addiction as an Attachment Disorder.* Lanham, MD: Jason Aronson.

Fonagy, P., G. Gergely, E. Jurist, and M. Target. 2004. *Affect Regulation, Mentalization, and the Development of the Self.* New York: Other Press.

Freud, A. 1996. *The Writings of Anna Freud, Vol. II, 1936: The Ego and the Mechanisms of Defense.* New York: International Universities Press.

Gal, R., and R. S. Lazarus. 1975. The role of activity in anticipating and confronting stressful situations. *Journal of Human Stress* 1:4-20.

Gallese, V., L. Fadiga, L. Fogassi, and G. Rizzolatti. 1996. Action recognition in the premotor cortex. *Brain* 119:593-609.

Goeders, N. E. 2004. Stress, motivation, and drug addiction. *Current Directions in Psychological Science* 13:33-35.

Goleman, D. 2006. *Social Intelligence: The New Science of Human Relationships.* New York: Random House.

Herman, J. L. 1992. *Trauma and Recovery: The Aftermath of Violence—From Domestic Abuse to Political Terror.* New York: Basic Books.

Hoffman, M. L. 2000. *Empathy and Moral Development: Implications for Caring and Justice.* Cambridge, UK: Cambridge University Press.

Horney, K. 1950. *Neurosis and Human Growth.* New York: Norton.

Izard, C. E. 1971. *The Face of Emotion.* Meredith, NY: Appleton-Century-Crofts.

Kohut, H. 1977. *The Restoration of the Self.* New York: International Universities Press.

————. 1984. *How Does Analysis Cure?* Chicago: The University of Chicago Press.

Lansky, M. R. 1994. Commentary on Andrew Morrison's The breadth and boundaries of a self-psychological immersion in shame. *Psychoanalytic Dialogues* 4:45-50.

Lazarus, R. S. 1999. Hope: An emotion and a vital coping resource against despair. *Social Research* 66 (2):653-678.

Lewis, T., F. Amini, and R. Lannon. 2000. *A General Theory of Love.* New York: Random House.

Lundqvist, L., and U. Dimberg. 1995. Facial expressions are contagious. *Journal of Psychophysiology* 9:203-211.

McWilliams, N. 1984. The psychology of the altruist. *Psychoanalytic Psychology* 1:193-213.

———. 1999. *Psychoanalytic Case Formulation.* New York: The Guilford Press.

McWilliams, N., and S. Lependorf. 1990. Narcissistic pathology of everyday life: The denial of remorse and gratitude. *Journal of Contemporary Psychoanalysis* 26:430-451.

Meltzoff, A., and M. K. Moore. 1977. Imitation of facial and manual gestures by human neonates. *Science* 198:75-78.

Morrison, A. P. 1983. Shame, the ideal self, and narcissism. *Contemporary Psychoanalysis* 19:295-318.

———. 1989. *Shame: The Underside of Narcissism.* New York: The Analytic Press.

Nathanson, D., ed. 1987. *The Many Faces of Shame.* New York: The Guilford Press.

Oswald, P. A. 1996. Effects of cognitive and affective perspective taking on empathic concern and altruistic helping. *Journal of Social Psychology* 136:613-623.

PDM Task Force. 2006. *Psychodynamic Diagnostic Manual (PDM),* Silver Spring, MD: Alliance of Psychoanalytic Organizations, 691-764.

Rizzolatti, G., L. Fadiga, V. Gallese, and L. Fogassi. 1996. Premotor cortex and the recognition of motor actions. *Cognitive and Brain Research* 3:131-141.

Ryan, R. M., V. I. Chirkov, T. D. Little, K. M. Sheldon, E. Timoshina, and E. L. Deci. 1999. The American dream in Russia: Extrinsic aspirations and well-being in two cultures. *Personality and Social Psychology Bulletin* 25:1509-1524.

Seelig, B. J., and L. S. Rosof. 2001. Normal and pathological altruism. *Journal of the American Psychoanalytic Association* 49:933-959.

Shamay-Tsoory, S. G., R. Tomer, B. D. Berger, and J. Aharon-Peretz. 2003. Characterization of empathy deficits following prefrontal brain damage: The role of the right ventromedial prefrontal cortex. *Journal of Cognitive Neuroscience* 15:324-337.

Sperling, M. B., and W. H. Berman. 1991. An attachment classification of desperate love. *Journal of Personality Assessment* 56:45-55.

Stets, J. E., and P. J. Burke. 2005. Identity verification, control, and aggression in marriage. *Social Psychology Quarterly* 68:160-178.

Swann, W. B. 1997. The trouble with change: Self-verification and allegiance to the self. *Psychological Science* 8:177-180.

Teicholz, J. G. 1998. Self and relationship: Kohut, Loewald, and the postmoderns. In *The World of Self Psychology: Progress in Self Psychology*, vol. 14, ed. A. Goldberg. Hillsdale, 267-292, Hillsdale, NJ: The Analytic Press.

van Dijke, M., and M. Poppe. 2006. Striving for personal power as a basis for social power dynamics. *European Journal of Social Psychology* 36:537–556.

Wangh, M. 1962. The "evocation of a proxy": A psychological maneuver, its use as a defense, its purposes and genesis. *Psychoanalytic Study of the Child* 17:451-469.

Weiss, J. 1993. *How Psychotherapy Works: Process and Technique*. New York: The Guilford Press.

Wurmser, L. 1981. *The Mask of Shame*. Baltimore: Johns Hopkins University Press.

Zaslav, M. R. 1998. Shame-related states of mind in psychotherapy. *Journal of Psychotherapy Practice and Research* 7:154-166.

Mary C. Lamia, Ph.D., is a clinical psychologist and psychoanalyst in private practice in Marin County, CA. She is also a professor at the Wright Institute in Berkeley, CA.

Marilyn J. Krieger, Ph.D., is a clinical psychologist in private practice in Marin County, CA.

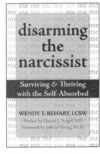